CAP & COMPASS

life after school. explained.

www.CapandCompass.com

Legal info

The authors of this book and Cap & Compass, LLC, have made their best efforts in preparing this book to be accurate and complete. The content of the book is not guaranteed to produce any particular result, but is for general informational purposes only. In addition, the advice and explanations given in the book may not fit every individual's circumstances.

Therefore, the authors and Cap & Compass, LLC, and Cap & Compass, Inc., do not assume responsibility for advice or information given. As a result, each reader should consider his or her specific circumstances when making decisions related to any of the topics covered in this book.

The authors and Cap & Compass, LLC, are not in the business of rendering legal, financial, or any other professional advice. If any questions regarding legal, financial, or professional advice should arise, the reader should seek professional assistance.

This book was updated in August of 2008.

Acknowledgements

life after school.
explained.

by the
Cap & Compass Writing Team

Jesse Vickey
Author, Founder

Andy Ferguson
Contributing Author

Nicole Vickey
Contributing Author, Co-Founder

Mark Harris
Humor contributor, Comic artist

The writing team at Cap & Compass extends thanks to everyone involved in making this book a finished product. This book is a collection of many people's experiences with life after school. The embarrassing and often funny stories told to us by friends, siblings, and seminar attendees have all made their way into these chapters. We greatly thank all those involved in the book, especially:

Jennifer Thomas-Hollenbeck
Ashley Manos
Randi Pierce
Editors

Maggie Bertish, Jason Butler, Bryan Knust, and Simeon Wallis
Contributors

We are also greatly indebted to the many students, recent graduates, parents, faculty members, work colleagues, tax accountants, insurance salesmen, apartment brokers, restaurant staff, investment advisors, and human resource managers who gave us advice, especially:

Jeff, Mark, Kate, Tom, Jane, Rob, Anne, Paul, Mary, Carolyn, Jerry, Sarah, Rob (another one), Megan, Angie, the Yalies who got a free pizza, Vinny, Janice, Val, Wu, Fruitz, Melinda, Kim, Alma, Dean Sue (cute picture), Jennifer N., Steve Blond, Ashley, Michael W., and anyone we're forgetting.

Thank you to Irene M Ward & Associates for help on the disability etiquette page. Find additional info at disabilitytraining.com or calling PDA at (800) 543-2119.

"That the powerful play goes on and you may contribute a verse. What will your verse be?"

– *John Keating*

Who is Cap & Compass?

We are a small, but growing company of young professionals who explain life after graduation. Cap & Compass offers three complementary products:

Seminars

We travel around the country presenting witty and informative seminars at college campuses, corporations, and conferences. These 45-minute seminars combine humor, audience participation, and creative visuals with serious information for succeeding in the "real" world. The five seminars are:

- Avoid Looking Stupid at Dinner
- Love Your Money
- Getting Your Apartment
- W4401kHMO: Translating Day 1 at Work
- The Least You Need to Know About Taxes

Books

In addition to the book you're reading, we publish these related titles:

- *the college years*
- *Graduating with God: for high school graduates*
- *Graduating with God: for college graduates*

All of our books use humor to help graduates with the "life skills" needed for their transition to life after school. See the next page for ordering details.

Starter kits

Cap & Compass offers starter kits for recent graduates moving to major cities like New York, Atlanta, LA, or DC. These on-line guides help with the apartment search, setting up utilities, obtaining a driver's license, getting a voter ID, and more.

Check them out on our company website:

www.CapandCompass.com

Cap & Compass was founded in 1999 by two young professionals, Jesse and Nicole Vickey, who felt that there should be an easier way to learn about life after school than by making mistakes on your own.

Purchasing this book

Individual copies

You can buy our books ONLINE for $12.95:

www.CapandCompass.com

If you're not into computers, feel free to CALL us to purchase the book:

(251) 476-1987

If you are opposed to computers and phones, you can buy one by MAIL. Please see the last page of this book for details.

Large quantities

Looking for the perfect senior gift or welcoming item for your young new hires? Our book is a fantastic promotional opportunity for schools and corporations. We offer the following customized options:

- **customize the cover**
  (color, photo, and logo)

- **customize the inside covers**
  (any message)

Customization is available on orders of 50 or more books. See our website for discounted bulk rates or e-mail us at:

Info@CapandCompass.com

Booking a seminar

If you're interested in bringing one of our humorous seminars to your campus, leadership conference, or business, please contact us at:

Info@CapandCompass.com

Visit our website for a full description of our five seminars:

www.CapandCompass.com

We usually present two of our 45-minute seminars on any given day per venue based on the interests of the hiring audience. Our seminar package is designed to be an affordable yet engaging choice for student programmers and human resources staff alike.

Table of contents

Table of Contents

Introduction

When you're in school, you learn how to draw demand curves, write about American politics, and diagram carbon atoms. Although these topics are important, they're not very helpful when you need to find an apartment, pick health insurance, or fill out your taxes. Who explains life after school?

Cap & Compass has created the definitive reference guide for life after school. You can read from cover to cover, or turn to the appropriate chapter as you reach your first business dinner, day on the job, tax season, or whatever.

This book was written with recent graduates in mind, but the topics are useful for anyone who eats, uses money, pays taxes, or works for a living.

We do not intend this book to be a substitute for the advice of professional accountants, financial advisors, apartment brokers, and so on. Rather, it is designed to help you get a basic understanding of the concepts and lingo. This foundation will help you have meaningful conversations with professionals to make the best decisions for you. So next time your HR manager wants to talk to you about your 401k or W-2, you'll have the decoder ring.

Throughout the book, you will see a little graduate guy. His name is Bert. He is a fictional character who is the subject of all of our  anecdotes and a front for all of our embarrassing stories. This book was compiled from the experiences of many recent graduates – our friends, our co-workers, our seminar attendees – plus professionals from many fields.

If you have feedback or ideas that would make this book better, we would love to hear from you. Please send us an e-mail at:

Info@CapandCompass.com

We hope you enjoy!

Seminar One

Avoid Looking Stupid at Dinner

Dracula's business dinner took a turn for the worst.

Avoid Looking Stupid at Dinner

Dinner overview

Snobby wines, odd food, and three different forks are the recipe for looking stupid. If you don't like to look stupid, then this chapter is for you.

Everyone knows a little bit about fancy dinners from authoritative sources like the movie *Pretty Woman*. Personally, we learned the finer points of mashed potato consumption from a student named Bluto who attended our seminar at Faber College.

Now we're going to take your working knowledge one step further. Since most people know what *not* to do at dinner, we'll tackle the stuff that you *should* do.

We'll cover etiquette issues and all the other things you'll need to know for a fancy meal. You'll get the inside skinny on the awkward wine presentation, learn fancy words like *foie gras,* and understand the dos and don'ts for different dishes, like sushi and steak.

We'll concentrate most of this chapter on the *business dinner,* but the ideas apply to any number of situations. Many job interviews, family gatherings, and most importantly, first dates take place over a nice dinner. No one likes to look like an idiot on the first date (unless you're *charming* as an idiot – everyone has their own bag of tricks). This chapter just may help you get a job *and* a love life.

Job success

85% people skills

15% technical skills

Everyone knows that "people skills" are important in the workplace. Some fancy research groups attempted to quantify this idea.

Harvard, Carnegie Foundation, and Stanford Research Center claim that 85% of your job success comes from your people skills, while only 15% comes from your technical skills and knowledge.

That's one reason why business dinners are so important.

Story time

Consider this story. Upon graduating from college, our good friend "Bert" took a job with a big consulting firm.

The company hosted a three-week orientation for Bert and the rest of the new hires. The orientation took place out of the office on a college campus.

During the three weeks of training, Bert attended classes during the day and dinners in the evening, followed by socializing once the day was done.

As company folklore now has it, Bert had a few too many drinks at dinner and kept right on drinking into the evening.

Bert's friend

Around 3 a.m., Bert and a friend thought it would be great fun to go for a dip in the fountain in the middle of campus.

Police apprehended the pair in their skivvies, and both were given the fast track to early retirement.

Once again, 85% of your job success is who you are, 15% is what you know.

The three golden rules

1) Not there to eat

Now, down to the business of decoding the business dinner.

Eating might be your number one priority, but it's not the number one priority of your boss. This is not a pie-eating contest.

A work dinner is a social occasion with an agenda.

A dinner may start a lasting relationship with a client or close an important business deal.

Relax, and remember the goals of the dinner while at the table.

2) Be discreet

If you're just out of school, you're invited to be part of the evening, not to be the star.

When we talked to human resource staff about new hires, they were always quick to mention:

"New hires try too hard to impress their colleagues."

Don't try to be an expert on company issues. Show that you are interested and informed, but don't call attention to yourself.

Everyone knows that you're relatively young and inexperienced. No one is going to care, unless you constantly remind them of this fact.

Your host is the person who decides to have the meal, invites the guests, and is usually called "boss" around the office. He or she will dictate how obnoxious the bill is going to be over the course of the meal.

Since you're not paying:

You need to follow the lead set by your host.

If you follow along well, you won't stand out from the crowd. (In this situation, that's good.)

Think of the dinner experience as one of those games you played in elementary school like Simon Says or Follow the Leader. (Weren't those the days?) Simon is the host, and you follow Simon's lead. We'll refer to the host as Simon over the course of this chapter.

If Simon orders dessert, you can order dessert. If Simon wants to jump out of a plane, strap on your parachute. If Simon wants to hang out and chat about Motown music, you make sure that you can't say enough about early Stevie Wonder.

"Early Stevie Wonder" would loosely be defined as the time period of 1963-1976.

Items worthy of discussion would include Stevie's early hits, such as "Fingertips, Part 2" and his concurrent first #1 album: *Recorded Live - The Twelve Year Old Genius.* This was followed by a string of hits: "Uptight (Everything's Alright)," "I Was Made to Love Her," and "My Cherie Amour," to name a few.

Additionally, marvel at Stevie's 15 Grammys, including three Album of the Year honors between 1973 and 1976.

Seating

Maitre D'

Most dinners start the same way. Someone escorts you to your table. Often, this person is called a Maitre D'. The Maitre D' is your welcoming presence at the restaurant.

Ladies, the "D" may pull your chair out for you to help you get seated. Gentlemen, the "D" may put your napkin on your lap. He's not trying to be fresh. Just say thank you and move on.

If you have any problems over the course of your meal, the "D" will help you out.

Do not call him "the 'D' " in front of your host. You'll look stupid.

Napkins

If the Maitre D' doesn't take care of your napkin, seize the moment and do so yourself.

Placing your napkin on your lap seems like such a simple thing to remember, but it's so easy to forget. After 15 minutes, you'll realize that everyone else has a napkin on his or her lap, and you still have an origami swan staring at you.

Also, your napkin should be on your lap at all times. If you need to excuse yourself at any point, put your napkin in your chair, not back on the table. A napkin on the table may be seen by your server as a signal that you're finished with your meal, and your plate may be taken.

Ignore the menu

Once you are seated, do not pick up the menu. Remember: This is not a pie-eating contest.

Talk to those around you. Create a comfortable atmosphere. You will be fed. You've made it to the restaurant; they've fed everyone who has ever shown up before. Chances are you won't break the streak.

Keep an eye on Simon. Once Simon picks up his or her menu, you can start looking at all of your free choices.

Small talk

"So I hear you color your hair."

You may not know many of the people at your table. In order to avoid an uncomfortable silence, prior to the meal, ask about the people joining you to find out a little about them. We don't suggest that you stalk them, but find out what they do or if they work with someone you know. This advice also applies to your dating life.

You also might want to freshen up on current events, sports, or other potential common interests.

Handshake

Once you introduce yourself, it's always nice to extend your hand. The proper handshake involves eye contact and a three-second firm grip. That's it. Anything else is hand jive and could be seen as too much.

Unfortunately, many people's handshakes can be classified into one of two categories:

The Fish: A limp shake with no eye contact.

The Gorilla: Not just a hand shake, but a signal that says: "I can break you."

Try to find a happy medium – say, a camel, or whatever.

Glasses & bread plates

Which glasses do you drink from?
The ones on your **right** or **left**?

You've said your hellos, taken your seat, and are ready to claim your bread plate and water glass. Unfortunately, all of the place settings are so close to each other that you don't know what is yours.

Your first step to *not* looking stupid is to remember this:

Glasses are on your right. Bread plate is on your left.

If anyone tries to use your glass or plate, tell them to back off.

Alternatively, place the blame on yourself and use the line, "I already used that glass to rinse my retainer."

An easy way to remember

imagine these are
your hands

your **left** hand forms a "**b**"
your **left** side is your **bread**

your **right** hand forms a "**d**"
your **right** side is your **drink**

To help you remember where to find your bread plate and glasses, hold your hands out in front of you and make "ok" signs. Use a little imagination, and you'll see a "b" for "bread" and a "d" for "drink" on your left and right hand, respectively.

But before you go around giving

the "double OK" or pretending like you're looking through binoculars at imaginary red-breasted whippoorwills, keep in mind that in some parts of the world this gesture is considered offensive. So, it's best to do it either discreetly under the table or simply in your mind -- you know, where the whippoorwills live.

Lipstick

Ladies, monitor your lipstick when going out on a work dinner. If you're wearing too much lipstick, you'll get the "Lips on the Glass" look, which scares people.

You're not a dog. You don't have to mark your territory by smearing lipstick all over your glass. If you're concerned about someone else drinking your wine, let the rest of the table see you backwash in your glass.

Gentlemen, under no circumstances should you ever have the "Lips on the Glass" look. Again, you want to *be discreet*.

The drink order

Now it's drink ordering time. If Simon doesn't order an alcoholic drink, you probably don't want to be drinking alcohol either.

Why? Remember, Simon sets the tone for the evening. The last thing you want to do is innocently order a glass of wine and have your boss glare at you from across the table.

You can't un-order the wine by saying, "Excuse me server, I didn't realize that was going to make me look like a moron. I'll just have iced tea."

Question for you

What if you're the <u>first</u> person asked to place a drink order, but you don't know what the protocol is?

Ladies, this could happen to you if you're the only woman at the table. Instead of simply ordering a non-alcoholic drink, here's an alternative:

Pass the buck.

Respond with the stock answer, "I don't know yet. Why don't you start with someone else?" Hopefully, this will allow you to find out what is appropriate and also send the message to the server: "Leave me alone. It's not my show." If your server gets the hint, he or she won't ask you first for the rest of the meal.

The basics of wine

In most cases, if you're out on a work dinner, the host will choose the wine.

If this is the case, once again, simply follow Simon's lead and indulge in his or her selection.

Occasionally, your colleagues may want to have a little bit of fun at your expense. They may think of you as young and naïve when it comes to wine and may ask *you* to order. We've been there before and will help you rise to the occasion.

Even if you're *not* asked to order, you should have some idea of what you're drinking.

As you may already know, wines come in many varieties. Wine is usually named after a grape, a region of the world, or a blend of grapes. The next page provides some examples that you may recognize.

You'll notice that none of the prominent regions in college wine circles are included here.

Next time you're at a restaurant with friends and you want to have a little fun, ask the server about his or her recommendations for wines from the Franzia or Boone's Farm region. If you're feeling particularly saucy, ask if any of the blended wines include the Mad Dog grape.

Grape

The following wines are named after types of grapes.

The quickest way to look stupid on a work dinner is to rhyme Merlot with "forgot." The pronunciations in the right-hand column should help you out.

Cabernet Sauvignon
         (cab-er-nay sav-in-yon)
Chardonnay   (shar-don-ay)
Merlot   (mer-low)
Pinot Grigio   (pee-no-gree-zhe-o)
Pinot Noir   (pee-no-n'war)
Reisling   (rees-ling)
Shiraz   (sure-oz)
Zinfandel   (zin-fan-del)

Region

These wines are named after particular regions of the world:

Beaujolais   (bo-zha-lay)
Bordeaux   (bor-doe)
Burgundy   (bur-gun-dee)
Chablis   (sha-blee)
Champagne   (hap-pee-nu-yeer)
Chianti   (key-awn-tee)
Port   (c'mon)
Sherry   (like the Journey* song)
*See page 182.

All of the above come from France, except Chianti (Italy), Port (Portugal), and Sherry (Spain).

Wines are often named after regions because the soil and climate of an area affect the grapes.

Neither

Occasionally, a wine won't be named after a grape or a region. A wine may be a blend, named after something completely extraneous to the grapes.

For example, the movie producer Francis Ford Coppola owns his own vineyard (show-off).

He created a wine, Talia Rose, that is a blend of a Coppola (we mean "couple of") different grapes, and named the wine after his *sister,* Talia, who enjoys Rose wines.

These wines often are called **branded** wines, **generic** wines, or wines with **proprietary names**. These were all created to make wine just a little more confusing.

Ordering wine

Red or white?

If you are asked to order the wine, don't stick your thumb in your mouth. Go ahead and take the bull by the horns.

The first thing you should ask the table is, "Would you like red or white?"

Sometimes you can make a decision based on the food your dinner companions will be eating.

beef, lamb, or pork = red wine
chicken or fish = white wine
pasta = match with sauce
(white with white, red with red)

Time for worries

So far, you've chosen the color. Nothing too complicated, right? Now things get a little more complex, and people begin to worry. How much can I spend? How do I know if I'm picking out a good one?

Price
Don't pick the least expensive wine. You'll look like you're making your selection based on price, when you should be making your selection based on wine. Don't go crazy, but be comfortable picking something a few rungs above the minimum. This will at least create the *impression* that you know what you're doing.

Knowledge

If you're the one picking the wine, this probably means that everyone else at the table doesn't know much more than you do. Choose with authority. Plus, the restaurant makes your job easy.

First, *the wine list is divided up by reds and whites,* and is subdivided into grapes or regions. If everyone wants a red, at least you'll be able to find a red.

Second, many fine restaurants will have a **wine steward**, or sommelier (som-mel-yay).

The wine steward will be the person who presents you with the wine list. The steward's job is to help you pick the right wine, so don't be afraid to ask questions.

In one suave sentence tell the steward your budget, your red/white preference, and maybe what you're eating. For example: **"Can you recommend a medium-priced red to go with my steak?"**

The best time to do this is when the wine steward's boss is in the area. Once the steward gives you an answer, respond loudly, "Wow! You are the most informative, customer-oriented wine steward ever!" This should improve your service for the rest of the night.

If you don't want to embarrass yourself with the pronunciation of a wine name, you are allowed to request the wine by **bin number**. A wine bin is where they keep the wines. "I'd like bin number 21, please."

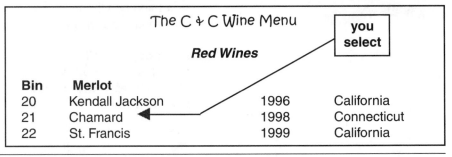

The C & C Wine Menu

you select

Red Wines

Bin	Merlot		
20	Kendall Jackson	1996	California
21	Chamard	1998	Connecticut
22	St. Francis	1999	California

The awkward wine presentation

Overview

The wine presentation can be intimidating initially, but once you know what you're doing, you'll look like a true wine snob.

These are all the different acts in the presentation:

See no evil.
(Check the label and vintage.)
Smell no evil.
(Smell the wine.)
Taste no evil.
(Taste the wine.)

The most important thing to remember about the presentation:

You are checking to see if the wine has gone *bad*.
You are not checking for *taste*.

See no evil

The first step in the awkward wine presentation is "See no evil."

The server or wine steward will present you with the bottle for your inspection.

You're supposed to check the label to see if he or she has gotten you the right bottle. Yes, occasionally servers have been known to screw up.

Determine if your server has brought you the correct bottle *before* he or she has a chance to open it. Once it's open, it becomes your bottle of wine, whether you like it or not (unless it's spoiled ... we're getting to that).

Most labels have basically the same information on them.

The **brand or winery** is where the wine was produced. The **cutsie picture** is intended for you to think, "Mmm, good wine! I should buy this one!" The **vintage** is *when* the grapes were harvested.

If a server is going to make a mistake, it's usually going to be with the vintage. You may have ordered a 1999 Chamard Merlot, but the bozo in the tie brought you a 1998.

You might think to yourself, "Who cares?" But the vintage is important.

Consider the story on the following page.

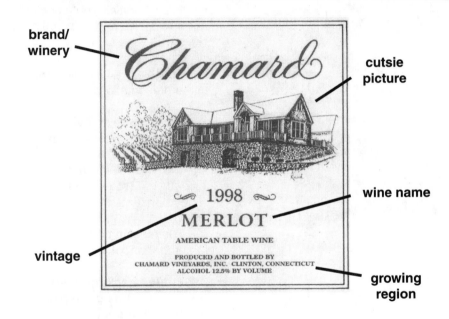

brand/winery

cutsie picture

wine name

vintage

growing region

The taste of a wine can vary from year to year for any number of reasons.

A particularly rainy year could cause mildew to form on the grapes, or the vineyard owner could become distracted from caring for his crop due to personal turmoil.

For instance, he could become obsessed with American Idol and forgo watering his grapes to catch the results show. But as he sits on the edge of his seat, cuddling his embroidered Clay Aiken pillow, waiting to hear who's being kicked off, Ryan Seacrest cuts to *another* commercial. Does Ford need to sell Focuses that badly?

Enraged, the vineyard owner throws his remote control into his plasma TV and kills it. Now he has no way to find out who won.

So, he hops into his truck (the irony of it being a Ford drives his rage even further) and heads to Hollywood. He arrives in time for the following week's results show, and as Seacrest is about to deliver another buzz-killing commercial break, the vineyard owner leaps on stage and holds him hostage with a corkscrew, demanding that he read the results on the spot.

You never know what happens from year to year. Make sure you always check the vintage. You don't want to pay $60 for a $2 bottle of wine.

Weather conditions can play an important role in the quality of wines produced in any given season (or **vintage year**). Weather obviously varies every year, which affects the taste of each year's grape crop. As expected, this impacts the quality of the wine. Prices vary accordingly.

Some wines do not carry a vintage on their label (creatively referred to as *nonvintage* **wines**). Although some people automatically consider these wines inferior, think otherwise.

There is no correlation between the quality of the wine and the presence of a vintage on a label. Nonvintage wines simply have grapes harvested from more than one year.

Next, the server will uncork the wine and pour a little bit in your glass.

The server will place the cork next to you. At this point, you'll need to eat the cork. Initially, the cork will taste dry, but after chewing it for a while, the saliva in your mouth will soften the texture.

If you don't like the taste of cork, you can put it in your mouth and *pretend to chew,* then spit it out in your napkin when no one is looking.

Actually, don't eat the cork. Don't even worry about smelling it.

You should smell the wine to see if it smells ok.

If it smells awful, like vinegar, then you know something is wrong.

Remember, your server is just going to pour a small amount in your glass, because the wine presentation is still in progress. Don't start hassling him with comments like, "Come on now, don't be stingy. Daddy's thirsty."

Comments like this could nullify the brownie points you accumulated earlier for the "you're the best wine steward ever" compliment. Your service might be average at best for the rest of the evening.

Now is a good time to mention the different wine glasses.

red wines   **white wines**

Red and white wines are served differently. Red wines are served at room temperature in fatter, shorter glasses. When you sip your red wine, don't say, "Someone left this out of the refrigerator for waaay too long."

White wines are served chilled in taller, thinner glasses.

Finally, you've come to the part in the presentation when you get to taste the wine.

After all, what's wine for if not to taste? Well, supposedly you can use white wine to get stains out of carpets. And red wine can be used to die fabrics. Also, if you let it sit out long enough, wine will turn into vinegar, and then you can use it as either a condiment or a household cleaner. We've even heard that some people in France blend parsley with wine to make a paste that heals bruises. And, of course, if you're rich enough, you can fill your pool and take a wine swim. But otherwise, it's for tasting.

As we mentioned earlier, you are not tasting to see if you *like* the wine. This is not an ice cream parlor. You are tasting to see if the wine is *spoiled*. Yes, every so often, a good wine goes bad.

Three things occasionally happen to wine:

- **the cork goes bad**
- **the grapes go bad**
- **air gets into the bottle**

Any of these things makes the wine disgusting and undrinkable. Imagine drinking something that tastes like a mixture of vinegar and the side of a barn.

Take just a *small* sip of wine, because the wine may be spoiled.

If you think this is the case, *do not spit your wine out into your neighbor's glass.* Act civilized and swallow the little bit of wine you have in your mouth. (In fact, the "No Spitting in Your Neighbor's Glass" rule is *always* in effect.)

Then, ask the person next to you to try the wine as well (in his or her own glass). If someone else agrees with you, tell the server that you think the wine is bad and that you'd like another bottle. Your server will be happy to replace it for you.

If the wine tastes ok, you should signal to the server that everything is fine. Your server will then fill everyone else's wine glass at the table and end by filling yours.

Ordering food

Now it's time to order. You look in your menu and panic when you don't see words like "pizza." You were allowed to ask about the wine, but you're not allowed to ask your server which dishes taste like chicken. We'll help you with this problem on the next page.

Also, at this point in the meal, you're all probably thinking one other thing when you look at the menu:

Sea Bass	**FREE**
Grilled Tuna	**FREE**
Grill of Game	**FREE**
Rack of Lamb	**FREE**

Yes, most business dinners mean free food for you. You'll be thinking to yourself, "What can I get away with?"

You'll probably order something that you don't usually try with your friends, but you still have to let good old Simon show you the way.

If Simon orders an appetizer, you should order an appetizer or a salad. Nothing is worse than watching a table of people eat. But if Simon only gets an entrée, you're probably out of luck ordering goose livers.

Speaking of goose livers, please see the following page.

Restaurants go out of their way to disguise the true nature of some of their ingredients. When you find out what all of these things actually are, you realize it makes sense for restaurants to use different names. It doesn't sound very appetizing to say, "I'll have the goose livers and fish eggs for myself, and please bring some airsick bags for the rest of the table."

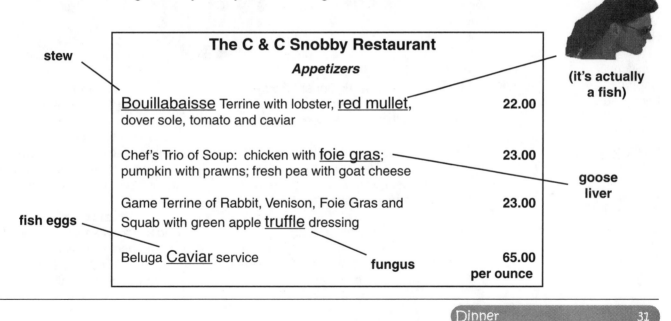

stew

fish eggs

(it's actually a fish)

goose liver

fungus

The C & C Snobby Restaurant

Appetizers

<u>Bouillabaisse</u> Terrine with lobster, <u>red mullet</u>, dover sole, tomato and caviar — 22.00

Chef's Trio of Soup: chicken with <u>foie gras</u>; pumpkin with prawns; fresh pea with goat cheese — 23.00

Game Terrine of Rabbit, Venison, Foie Gras and Squab with green apple <u>truffle</u> dressing — 23.00

Beluga <u>Caviar</u> service — 65.00 per ounce

The list is infinite, but here are a couple of other words that might pop up on a menu:

Chiles	hot peppers
Morels	brain-like fungus
Rhubarb	stalk of a plant (leaves are toxic)
Venison	Bambi
Capers	flower bud
Fricassee	stew
Tartare	raw
Escargot	snails
Ceviche	raw fish
Gnocchi	potato dumplings
Vermicelli	thin spaghetti
Arugula	salad green
Carpaccio	raw beef
Leek	onion
Turbot	fish
Parsnip	root

sushi

rolls (maki)

If your work dinner takes you to a sushi restaurant, these are the basic things you'll need to know:

Sushi
Raw fish (you'll have many choices) over rice is commonly referred to as sushi.

Rolls (Maki)
Rolls are raw fish or some other food item (like cucumber) wrapped in rice and seaweed.

Sashimi
This is raw fish without the rice.

Wasabi
Wasabi is a *very* spicy horse-radish that looks like green Play-Doh (but it's certainly not child's play).

What to do
Add a *little* wasabi to the top of your maki. Using chopsticks, dip your food in the soy sauce and then your mouth. Chew. Swallow. Smile.

Steaks

Here's the part of the book that gets the vegetarians all excited. If you go out on a few work dinners, you'll inevitably wind up at a steakhouse.

When you go to a steakhouse, you already know what you're going to get as a main dish: steak. But there is still plenty to decide. Steakhouses are famous for their variety of cuts of meat. This is what you need to know:

Meat is muscle. Unexercised muscle is tender. People like their meat tender.

Therefore, the best (and most expensive) pieces of meat come from the parts in the cow that are least exercised.

Take a look at the diagram on the following page.

The Cap & Compass Steakhouse

Filet
Cut generously, broiled expertly to melt-in-your mouth tenderness.
23.95

Ribeye
Well-marbled for peak flavor, deliciously juicy.
23.50

Porterhouse for Two
Combines the rich flavor of the strip with the tenderness of the filet.
25.95 per person

Tofu Steak
Order this and you'll be removed from our restaurant.
26.95

Chuck the cow*

*See page 182.

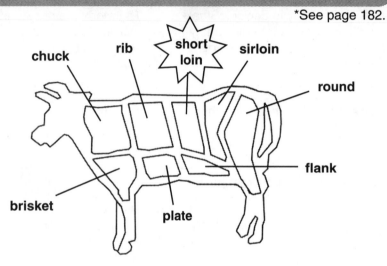

chuck • rib • short loin • sirloin • round • flank • plate • brisket

This is Chuck, our friendly cow. Chuck never visits the local gym. He simply walks around all day eating grass. Therefore, the muscles around his legs are tough, while the short loin area (away from the legs) is most tender. Now you're a cow expert.

Most steaks in a steakhouse come from the short loin (porterhouse, T-bone, filet, and NY strip).

Steak math

What are the differences in the meats? Surprisingly, many are alike. To see this, you'll have to do a little bit of "steak math":

$$\text{T-bone or Porterhouse} = \text{Filet + NY Strip}$$

$$\text{Rib Eye} = \text{Prime Rib}$$

T-bone and porterhouse are each made up of two pieces of meat: a filet and a strip (one on each side of the bone). The porterhouse has a bigger filet than the T-bone.

Rib eye and prime rib are the same cuts of meat, just cooked differently. The rib eye is grilled while the prime rib is slow roasted.

Only the best

If you remember one thing, remember that the **filet mignon** is usually the least exercised, most tender, and most expensive (per ounce) piece of meat. If you're out on the company bill and Simon leads you to the expensive side of the menu, give the filet a chance.

Men, if your girlfriend ever gives you a hard time for looking "tender" and doughy (maybe you haven't visited the gym in a while), you should make her stop chastising you and demand that she treat you like a *fine piece of filet mignon.*

"Chewing the cud"

Have you ever heard the expression "chewing the cud" when a number of people are sitting around talking about nothing? Have you ever wondered what that meant?

Apparently, cows have numerous stomachs. When a cow eats grass, it swallows its food into stomach number one. After a while, the cow *regurgitates* this food *back into its mouth.* The cow then re-eats this "grass" and swallows it again into a different stomach. That's disgusting. That's "chewing the cud."

Wait, maybe the expression is "chewing the fat." Anyways.

Close your menu

Now back to the topic at hand. Up until now, things have been flowing pretty smoothly. You've got your drink, you've made up your mind about the food and appetizers, and you're ready to order.

One problem. You've got to:

Close your menu!

It seems so obvious, but if you leave it open, the server is never going to come to your table.

When people start complaining about the service and then notice your menu still open, they're going to throw silverware at you.

Silverware

When the food arrives, you're going to look down at your place setting and see an ocean of silverware before you. This diagram will help you navigate the high seas.

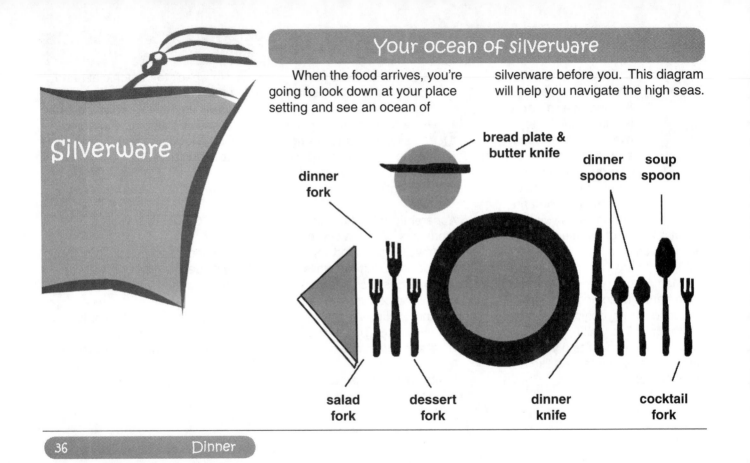

bread plate & butter knife

dinner fork

dinner spoons

soup spoon

salad fork

dessert fork

dinner knife

cocktail fork

Silverware review

When figuring out your silverware, here's your rule of thumb:

Work from the outside in.

The first courses will use the outer silverware.

Also, never allow used silverware to rest on the table. It should always be on your dish.

Also remember:

Butter knife and plate
You should always "butter your plate" first and use this butter for your bread. You want to avoid continually returning to the original butter. "Can you pass the butter ... *again* ... please?"

Tear off bite-sized portions of your bread, and only butter these portions as you eat them.

If you start the bread, offer a piece to the person on your right and then pass the bread to your left. In general, pass things to the left.

Soup spoon and bowl
Your soup spoon is giant, because everyone should feel like an ogre eating porridge at least once in their life.

When you come to the bottom of your bowl, tilt the bowl away from you to get the last of your soup.

If you hate your fellow diners, slurp as loudly as possible, belch, then turn to your neighbor and say, "Soup good. Me finished."

Tea spoons
If you have two tea spoons (as in the diagram on the page to the left), the *outside* spoon is reserved for throwing, not the inside spoon. If you throw the inside spoon, you'll look foolish in front of everyone else at the table. Actually, we can't find any good reason for a second spoon other than pretention.

Bite-sized portions

Make a conscious effort to eat bite-sized portions. Otherwise, you'll be forced into an uncomfortable 30-second pause when asked a question.

Finished eating

Once you've finally finished eating, you should put your silverware on your plate, fork tongs down, in this position (roughly 4 o'clock). Servers are actually trained to look for this.

In case you're wondering, they are also trained to ask you a question when your mouth is full or during a marriage proposal.

Generally speaking, you are not allowed to ask for a doggie bag when out on a business dinner.

Granted, the food may have been great and free, but again, you don't want to call attention to yourself on the work dinner. "Hi everybody. I'm poor. I get to eat this for lunch tomorrow!"

Instead, eat so much that you feel like you won't have to eat for another three days.

Business dinners are notorious for lasting a long time. Once the meal is over, get comfortable and take your cues from Simon.

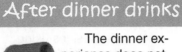

After dinner

The dinner experience does not end when the food is taken from the table. After dinner drinks are important. This is your chance to "wow" everyone without resorting to your meticulous recreation of the Battle of Gettysburg using dinner rolls, toothpicks, and your stash of stolen McDonald's ketchup packets.

When it's time to order,

you need to have something to say.

Talk to your friends or try a couple drinks yourself before the big dinner. That way, when the time comes, you'll fit right in.

Examples

Port wine
Port wines are sweeter than normal wines and are rarely consumed *during* the meal. Their alcoholic content is greater than most regular wines.

Whisky
Whisky is a liquor made from grain. **Scotch** (from Scotland) and **bourbon** (from Bourbon County, Kentucky) are both types of whisky.

Scotch
There are two kinds of Scotch: **single malts** (they come from one distillery) such as Glenlivet and Glenfiddich, and **blends** such as Chevis Regal, J&B, and Dewar's. Scotch snobs like single malts.

Brandy

Brandy is a liquor distilled from wine. **Cognac** (from Cognac, France) is a type of brandy.

Liqueur

A liqueur is a sweetened alcoholic drink. All liqueurs taste much more "alcoholic" than indicated in the simple descriptions below. (You'll have to test them.)

Name	Flavor
Amaretto	almond
Bailey's	chocolatey cream
Chambord	raspberry
Cointreau	orange
Crème de Menthe	peppermint
Frangelico	hazelnut
Grand Marnier	slightly orange
Kahlua	coffee
Sambuca	licorice candy

Besides using manners, another way to distinguish yourself at a business dinner is to send a thank-you to your host for inviting you to dinner.

This may not always be appropriate when the host was your immediate boss (you brown-noser), but a thank-you is important if a client was the host. This simple gesture can go a long way.

No one ever got into much trouble for being too thoughtful. Unless, of course, you turn up on their doorstep at two in the morning professing your undying love with a handful of your baby teeth. A letter will do just fine.

The business dinner can be a very enjoyable experience if you remember the three most important rules:

You're not there to eat.
Be discreet.
Follow the lead of your host.

You're only at this meeting because Simon wants you there. Think of this as a compliment. Simon obviously likes you and wants you around. So relax and be yourself (unless, of course, "yourself" is a belligerent alcoholic).

Seminar Two

Love Your Money

Ted's credit card debt had gotten out of hand.

Love Your Money

Love it! Squeeze it! Kiss it! Your money deserves better than a cheap motel room. Give it roses by learning how to *Love Your Money*.

You'll find the roses in three sections within this chapter:

Bringing it in
This section explains your investment choices.

Giving it away
You'll learn the most common places you pay interest.

Uniting the *Love*
This section brings tips from the first two sections together, so you can really Love Your Money.

A few easy decisions here and there can lead to a few extra hundred dollars in your pocket each year.

Your relationship is even sweeter with this money because you don't have to work for it. Isn't that the best kind of *Love*? You just have to make some smart decisions.

Everyone has a different level of knowledge when it comes to money. We'll provide nuggets of information for people who understand the ins and outs of the P/E ratio, as well as for those just beginning to master the intricacies of the ATM.

We'll share *Love* with everyone.

Before we dig in, let's start off with a story.

This is a story about our good friend, Bert. Bert had a credit card that didn't pay him any rewards, and he only paid the minimum balance each month. He ended up paying an interest rate on his credit card ten times what he was earning on his savings account. That's certainly not *Love*. Bert graduated from school with tremendous debt.

To make money, Bert began donating his body to science. He got paid for a variety of medical experiments -- at first, relatively harmless cold studies, but eventually leading up to cutting-edge genetic research. Within a few months, he'd grown a third ear and a prehensile tail.

The extra ear came in handy one day when Bert heard a kitten mewing from the branches of a tree. Using his prehensile tail, he climbed the tree and rescued the cat. He was immediately hailed in the local paper as a superhero of some sort: Extra Ear Guy With a Tail.

However, that drew the attention of the local union of super villains -- Dark Breath, Sinister Boots, the whole gang -- who were threatened by the presence of a new nemesis. They kidnapped Bert, dangled him over a vat of boiling oil, and were about to drop him when they realized that his powers -- the ability to hear twice as well on the left side of his head while pouring a cup of coffee without using his hands -- were far from super.

They decided to let him go with just a villainous group noogie. Bert has been in therapy ever since.

This is, of course, just one example of what can happen to you. Individual results vary.

So... Bert's life never turned out the way he dreamed, because he never learned to *Love* his money.

Don't end up like Bert. In the next few pages, we'll show you how to get the *Love*.

Before we discuss the nitty-gritty of money, we need to talk about the basics. Granted, this stuff is very simple, but it sets a good foundation for later.

The **Rule of Money** (that's what we'll call it) says:

> **When you use someone else's money, you have to pay for it.**

For example, when you make a deposit in the bank, the bank uses your money. They have to pay for it. They pay you **interest**.

When you borrow money to pay for college, you are using someone else's money. You have to pay for it. You pay your lender **interest**.

The most important thing to understand is that the "interest" you earn is the same kind of interest as the "interest" you pay (simple enough).

Put another way, the relationship goes *both ways*. You *earn* interest when someone else uses *your* money, and you *pay* interest for the use of *someone else's* money.

Now you're certainly "interested." Ba-dum Ching! Thanks folks. You've been a lovely audience. Don't forget to tip your waitress.

Bringing it in

First let's talk about "Bringing it in." We're not talking about your salary. We're referring to bringing in money *without* doing any work, **earning interest**. This section is about someone paying you for the use of your money.

We'll explain the pros and cons of six of the most popular places you can keep your money:

- **Nowhere**
- **Checking**
- **Savings**
- **CDs**
- **Money market funds**
- **Stocks / mutual funds**

We found Bankrate.com a good source for interest rates.

In our seminars, we always ask people where they tend to keep their money.

Overwhelmingly, everyone answers "checking account" or "savings account." Occasionally we'll hear, "In a new Xbox 360!!" which is usually followed by an elbow to a friend and a "Good one, eh?"

Our best answer came from a gentleman sitting in the back row, who responded, "In my girl's wallet." She was sitting next to him and responded on cue, "Mmm-hmm."

We know how you feel.

Bringing it in:

Nowhere

Putting your money in your wallet or under your mattress requires no effort and no planning. Your cash will sit there and soak up the rays of your financial apathy.

Although this "investment" of yours won't lose any money, you won't earn any money either. Since this isn't 1865, you shouldn't fear outlaws robbing your bank and taking everything you own. You don't have to hide your money behind a picture on the wall.

Assuming that you're aiming higher in life, let's move on to some of the other choices.

Summary

Pros

You won't lose your money *(unless you forget under which mattress you stashed it).* Your money's always available.

Cons

You won't earn any interest – ever. This proves you're lazy. Your money won't be worth as much over time (word for econ geeks: inflation).

Conclusion

No *Love.* Don't be a couch potato.

Bringing it in:

Checking accounts

Everybody knows about checking accounts. Everybody loves checking accounts.

Here's the problem: Basic checking accounts usually pay **0% interest**.

The bank gets to use your money, but doesn't pay you for it. As you now know, that is *not fair*. The Rule says:

When you use someone else's money, you have to pay for it.

A checking account is using your money and not paying for it. That's breaking the Rule.

To make matters worse, checking accounts often charge *you* a monthly fee. Let's get this straight: *You* pay the fee, and *they* use your money.

Checking accounts are like deadbeat roommates. They eat your food, use up your hot water, delete your favorite shows from TiVo (to make room for Jerry Springer), and then ask you to cover them for their half of the rent. That's not *Love*.

Some banks will advertise "free checking," meaning you aren't charged fees. But they're still using your money for free. So who really wins?

Checking overview

One way to *Love Your Money* is to keep a *minimal* amount of your money in your checking account.

Everybody needs to write a check or visit an ATM once in a while. Checking accounts are a needed service. But you should only keep enough money in there to cover your checks and any minimum balance required by your bank.

Checking accounts don't play fair on the playground, so only play with them when absolutely necessary.

Summary

Pros

You have easy access to your money.
You can write checks.
You can go to ATMs.

Cons

You earn zero interest.
You might be charged fees.

Conclusion

No *Love*.
Don't play with bullies.

Designer checks

When you open a checking account, you will be faced with one of life's most difficult decisions: plain checks or the cool ones with Snoopy on them? Expect to pay a little more for the designer checks. Also consider these points when ordering:

Kitten checks: These say, "I have two dozen cats and zero dozen dates."

Cute baby checks: These say, "If I don't already have kids, I'm looking to have some. Now."

Winnie the Pooh checks: These say, "I might be eight years old."

Bringing it in:

Savings accounts

Savings accounts are like Paris Hilton: Once you get past the surface, there isn't a whole lot of substance. (Our apologies to the Paris Fan Club.)

Here's why: basic savings accounts pay squat. Uncle Sam may guarantee your money, but a savings account often only pays you 1-2% interest. That's not *Love*.

While 1-2% is better than the bully checking accounts, you have better alternatives. You'll find out about those soon.

Another way to *Love Your Money* is to avoid savings accounts.

Summary

Pros

Easy access to your money. You can go to ATMs.

Cons

You earn 1-2% interest.

Conclusion

No Love.
Think *The Hottie and the Nottie*.

Bringing it in: CDs

You're probably thinking to yourself, "CDs? I *love* the Chunichi Dragons. Hidenori Kuramoto is *such* a dreamboat." Actually, we're talking about Certificates of Deposit. These are places you invest your money for *set periods of time*.

Each CD has a set life span (3 months up to 10 years) with a set interest rate. When you put your money in a CD, you have to keep it there. Your money is in prison, and there are *no conjugal visits*.

For example, if you put $1000 into a one-year CD at 3%, you'll be guaranteed to earn $30 interest after a year. You lock in the 3% rate.

If you take your money out early, you'll get whacked with a big penalty (which negates the reason for having put your money there in the first place).

You are rewarded for putting your money in prison (we're going to pass on the opportunity for prison jokes here) by earning more interest.

CDs usually pay more than savings accounts.

The rates will change according to the prison sentence of 3 months, 6 months, or whatever. Most banks have cute little signs in their lobbies showing the most recent rates.

Usually, the interest rate will

CDs overview (cont.)

be higher, the longer the sentence. Rates can vary widely from bank to bank, so shop around.

If you need access to your money, avoid CDs. Coming out of school, you may have a lot of initial expenses and need access to cash. The minimum deposit for a CD is usually around $1000, but this amount varies from bank to bank.

But if you don't need your money for a set period of time and you want to lock in a rate, a CD might be a good, safe option for storing your cash. Just make sure that you won't need this money during its prison term.

Summary

Pros

Slightly better rates than checking or savings accounts. You lock in your rate. CDs are usually guaranteed by the government.

Cons

Your money is in prison. You'll pay penalties for taking your money out early.

Conclusion

So-so *Love*. Your money is in prison.

Seminar moment

At this point, we used to jokingly ask the audience, "So who here has been to prison? Someone must have a good story."

Usually this question prompted someone to tell a harmless story about how some friends went toilet-papering, got caught, went to jail, and their parents picked them up. We'd laugh and move on.

We stopped asking that question when someone responded, "Yes, I've been there a number of times. I tutor inmates on their literacy skills."

Hilarious.

We learned to *not* make the questions too open-ended.

Bringing it in:

Money market funds

We've been promising *Love* and here it is. You're not going to end up like Bert.

A money market fund is the Elvis Presley of safe investments. This choice is the King, because it pays you more than a savings account *and* allows you to write checks. Here are some of the benefits:

High rates
Money market funds almost always pay higher interest rates than savings accounts, and usually higher than CDs. In 2008, many funds paid around 3% (historically a fairly low rate).

Easy access
Your money is *never in prison,* like when you invest in a CD. You may not be able to use an ATM to get your money, but many money market funds allow you to zap your money into your checking account in a day's time for no fee.

Low-risk *Love*
Money market funds are extremely safe *Love.* Think of loving a puppy, or whatever.

Check writing
With many money market funds, you can even write checks. Is this financial utopia?

Pretty close. There are a couple of minor drawbacks. See the next page.

Rates move around

You may put your money into the fund earning 5%, but after six months, the rate may drop to 3% or jump to 9%. You cannot lock in your rate. However, these rates are still usually higher than savings account rates.

No government guarantee

The government does not guarantee money market funds, so *theoretically,* you could lose your money. But no US money market fund has *ever* lost money. You can't find a much safer investment.

Big checks

If you write a check, it usually has to be a BIG check (often $250 or more). When you need to pay rent or make a loan payment, a money market fund is perfect. For making smaller purchases, you'll still need a checking account.

Minimum deposits

A few have a $1000 minimum to open an account, but most are closer to $2500. But most other investments have minimums, too.

Not at banks

You *usually* can't get money market funds in your local bank. They'll offer something called money market *accounts,* but those often pay the same rates as savings accounts (ask your bank for all of their high interest rate options).

Much like finding your soulmate, it's easiest to buy a money market fund on the Internet.

Step 1: Go to a mutual fund site. These are the biggest four:

Vanguard Group
Putnam Investments
Fidelity
American Funds

Most money market funds will pay fairly similar rates, but you should still shop around. You may find a few without the check-writing capability that pay higher rates.

Step 2: Once you've found a site, you'll want to pick "mutual funds" from your list of choices.

Step 3: Mutual funds are usually subdivided into different categories (equity funds, bond funds, and money market funds).

Getting one (Cont.)

You'll obviously want to pick "money market funds."

Make sure you arrive prepared, because you'll have to remember things like your name and address. You can refer to your driver's license for these.

So as a quick recap, a great way to *Love Your Money* is to use money market funds. They are a better choice than checking accounts, savings accounts, or CDs, because they pay well, provide check-writing capability, and allow you access to your money. They're the King.

Summary

Pros

Money market funds offer some of the best rates for low-risk investments. You can write checks. Your investment is safe.

Cons

Rates move. You must write big checks. Money market funds have minimum investments.

Conclusion

This is Love. They're like Elvis: The King.

Side note

You may be thinking to yourself, "2% … 3% … 6% … What's the big deal?"

Consider this: If you invest $1000 in something that pays you 6% versus 2%, you'll earn $60 by the end of the year versus $20.

You are not doing *any* work to earn this extra money, except simply making a decision about where to put it. If someone offered you $40 for doing nothing, wouldn't you take it?

Lay the foundation. If you *Love Your Money* now when you're making small change, you'll see a big difference when you're making the seven-figure salary.

Up until now, we've been looking at *safe* places to put your money.

Now you're entering the world of *high-risk Love*. Investments in stocks and mutual funds come at the real risk of losing money – and not just your 2% or 6% interest. Your entire investment could go into the toilet.

Historically speaking, "the market" has done well. If you look at this graph below, you can see that if you had invested in the *general* market for a decade, you'd have been a winner.

But even during this "up" period of ten years, you could have easily lost your money during *short* periods of time.

Bringing it in:

Stocks & mutual funds

Dow Jones
Industrial Average
(10 year period)

loss in the short term

Additionally, had you invested in a single stock during this "up" decade, you could have come up a loser (financially – not necessarily in real life).

During the past ten years, many stocks either went belly-up or declined. Below is an example of a transportation stock during that same ten-year period.

Generally speaking, the market is a great investment over the long term. But *individual* stocks or *short-term* investments can leave you poor and sad.

There are two large avenues for investing in the market: stocks and mutual funds. You'll see that the two are very similar.

When you buy the **stock** of a company, you're actually buying *part* of that company (but don't expect to own the corner office with the nice view). You own a small, small sliver. If you buy ten ba-zillion shares, you own a medium-sized sliver.

If the company does well, the stock will probably do well, and you'll be able to buy yourself a nice new watch. If the CEO of the company is a crook and robs the company dry, then you may have to visit the local pawn shop and try to get your money back.

So, owning a stock implies part ownership of a company.

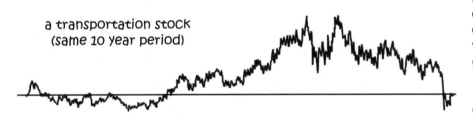

a transportation stock
(same 10 year period)

Mutual funds definition

A **mutual fund** is just a whole bunch of stocks, bonds, or some-things put into a nice little bundle. For instance, one fund might be a bunch of food or tech stocks.

Imagine if Cap & Compass were a mutual fund company (not yet, but maybe one day). We might have a Food Fund or a Tech Fund. Each fund would invest only in food or technology companies. You'd never really know which stocks were in each fund at any given time. *Fund investments continually change.*

Mutual funds are generally considered "safer" than individual stocks, because when some stocks in a fund go down, others *may* go up to offset each other.

The important thing to remember is that when you buy a mutual fund, you are allowing *someone else* (a **mutual fund manager**) to make your investment decisions for you.

If this section is boring you, please refer to page 174.

Cap & Compass Funds	
C & C Food Fund	**C & C Tech Fund**
Heinz	Cisco
Kraft Foods	Intel
Campbell Soup	Microsoft

Story time

Picking stocks is a lot like picking horses. So we'll tell a horse track story.

Once upon a time, our good friend Bert spent all his time at the horse track.

He looked in the program through mounds of information that meant nothing to him and then picked a horse named Bobby Blue Shoes, because the name sounded cool. (Word of advice: Don't pick stocks because the name sounds cool.) Occasionally, he'd pick the first horse that peed before the race, because it made the horse "lighter."

Bert continued to use his sophisticated gambling methods until he lost the first three races on which he bet. Obviously, something wasn't working.

He looked through the rest of the program and noticed an ad for "Race Track Eddie's Pick of the Week!" All he had to do was call up Eddie's 1-900 number and pay $4 a minute for his advice.

Bert thought, "I've seen Eddie before. He's that *classy* guy I always see smoking cigars and flirting with the horses and calling them his 'ladies.' He *must* know what he's talking about." So Bert called him at $4 per minute.

Buying a mutual fund is like calling Race Track Eddie. You're paying *someone else* to pick your investments for you.

Race Track Eddie's "Pick of the Week" might make you money, but it might not. You pay a fee for Eddie's advice either way. The same holds true for mutual funds.

Give Eddie a degree from Harvard, change his name to Warren, and that's your **mutual fund manager**. You pay a fund manager to pick some stocks for you. Your manager might be right. Or might not. But you're going to pay a fee for the advice either way.

Let's say we're hiring Race Track Warren to run the Cap & Compass Food Fund. If you decide that you want to invest in food stocks, you can buy our fund, and Warren will make your individual investment choices.

Once again, you'll know that your investments are in the food sector, but you won't know which specific companies you own at any given moment. If you knew this information, you could make these investments yourself and bypass Warren and his fees.

Hopefully, his decisions will be more informed than picking the first stock that pees before the race. Wait, now we're getting the two characters in our story mixed up.

As we mentioned, mutual fund companies need to make their fees. The government might frown upon 1-900 numbers, so they hide these fees in other ways.

Many times these fees are called **loads**. A mutual fund may charge you a **front-end load** or a **back-end load.** We considered using a few celebrity-reference jokes here, but voted against it. You figure it out.

Front-end load

Front-end loads get charged to you before the race even gets started. Assume that the load is 2%. If you give Warren $1000 to invest, you lose $20 before the race starts. Avoid them.

Back-end load

Back-end loads get charged when you *withdraw* your money from the fund. Avoid these fees, too.

Alternatives

Not all funds charge loads, so why buy these funds?

You don't have to buy **load funds**. In fact, there's no evidence that funds with loads perform better than funds with no loads.

But of course, you have to be charged somewhere. That's where the **expense ratio** comes in. (Almost all funds charge this.)

Expense ratio

An expense ratio is a pay-as-you-go fee, much like a 1-900 number. If a fund has a 2% annual expense ratio, you'll only pay that expense for the number of days your money is in the fund. If you own the fund for half a year, you'll only get charged half the fee, or 1%.

These fees pay the college tuition for Warren's kids and his swimming pool out back (with a diving board) – plus advertising and printing costs.

The expense ratio is pretty much unavoidable. But many funds are **no-load funds** with the only fee being the expense ratio.

Up until now, when we've talked about mutual funds, we've talked about *stock* mutual funds. When you go to buy your first mutual fund, you'll notice that you can buy a **bond fund**, too. Can you stand the excitement?!

Bonds are IOUs.

When a company or government (like the US government) needs a little extra money to buy chocolate malts for the ladies at the soda shop, they issue bonds (or IOUs) to get some cash.

The Rule of Money states:

When you use someone else's money, you have to pay for it.

These companies or governments need to pay back their money with interest. So how much interest do they have to pay?

That all depends on you: *At what rate would you feel comfortable enough to give up your money with the chance of not getting it back?* Your answer should depend on who is borrowing your money.

If you lend your money to Uncle Sam (the US government), you should feel pretty confident that you'll get your money back.

Suppose your cousin Tommy starts a company that sells gift wrap that looks like newspaper. *(Think about this for a second.)* You might not feel as safe giving money to his

company, which might go belly-up in a month.

In order to give up your money to Tommy, you'd need to get paid a higher interest rate to feel comfortable.

That's how bonds work, in a nutshell. Safe borrowers (like Uncle Sam) issue bonds for low rates, while riskier companies or governments (like your cousin Tommy) issue IOUs for higher rates of interest.

When you buy a *bond* mutual fund, determine whether these bonds are issued by safe or sketchy companies. Bonds can rise and fall just like stocks. Get to know where you put your money.

Indexes and ETFs

So now you want to get your hands on some mutual funds, but you don't know which group of stocks, or **sector**, to put them in. Food? Technology? Who knows?

You may want to invest in a broad mix of stocks, because as we mentioned earlier, the general market usually does well over time.

How do you do this?

For starters, it's difficult to keep track of every stock in the world (for most of us), so when people refer to "the market" they usually mean one of the **indexes** below. The Dow Jones, Nasdaq, and S&P 500 are intended to represent the whole market.

You've probably seen these names in the news every day. If not, *watch the news.*

In order to invest in an index, you can do one of two things:

- **Buy an index mutual fund**
- **Buy an ETF**
  (exchange-traded fund)

Index	Description	Big stocks	ETF
Dow Jones Industrial Avg	30 of the biggest companies in the US	3M, IBM, Proctor & Gamble	DIA (Diamonds)
Nasdaq	5000+ companies (many in technology)	Cisco, Intel, Microsoft	QQQQ (for Nasdaq 100)
S&P 500	500 widely held companies	GE, Intel, Cisco	SPY (SPDRs = "Spiders")

An **index mutual fund** is a fund that mimics the performance of an index. If the index rises 1%, your fund will rise 1%. But you'll still have to pay Warren some fees.

An **ETF** does the same thing, but usually with lower fees.

The **DIA**, **QQQQ**, and **SPY** are stocks that track different indexes. These ETFs can be purchased like any other stock from an on-line broker.

If you're looking for an easy way to invest in the general market with minimal fees, an ETF (DIA, QQQQ, or SPY) is a good start.

The easiest way to buy stocks is to purchase them on-line. These are some **on-line brokers:**

Charles Schwab	schwab.com
E*Trade	etrade.com
Fidelity	fidelity.com
Scottrade	scottrade.com
Sharebuilder	sharebuilder.com
TD Ameritrade	tdameritrade.com

Shop around. The fee charged for each transaction can vary dramatically (from $5 to over $40). Often, you'll find a trade-off between price and the availability of stock research information.

As mentioned earlier, stocks represent high-risk *Love*. If you invest for the short term, be willing to handle large price swings in your investment.

Also be aware that stock prices are largely driven by *expectations,* among other things. If you find a company that you feel is strong or weak, determine whether your opinions have already been factored into the price of the stock.

Many stocks fall on positive earnings reports (every quarter, companies announce how things are going), because *expectations* of the company's earnings were even higher than the earnings reported.

Buying mutual funds

You can also purchase mutual funds through on-line brokers, like the ones we mentioned earlier, but an on-line broker is usually a more expensive option.

Avoid the middleman by buying funds directly through a **mutual fund family**. Some of your choices include:

AmericanFunds americanfunds.com
Blackrock   blackrock.com
Fidelity   fidelity.com
Janus   janus.com
Putnam   putnam.com
T. Rowe Price   troweprice.com
Vanguard   vanguard.com

Purchase one of a gazillion mutual fund magazines (with once creative titles like *Mutual Fund Magazine*) for rankings and information on funds and their past performances.

When making your decisions, keep in mind that mutual funds are often romanticized as great investments, because some smart person invests your money for you, and you're buying a mix of stocks.

When you buy a technology fund, you're still investing in technology *stocks*. If all technology stocks go down (which, amazingly, has been known to happen), your fund also will go down.

Don't be lulled into a false sense of security just because you have Warren on your side.

Fund choices

When you buy a mutual fund, these terms will help:

Growth funds: These funds are usually composed of companies that still have growth potential.

Income funds: The companies in these funds are more established and make periodic payments.

Balanced funds: These funds mix stocks and bonds.

Also, **large-cap** or **blue-chip** stocks represent large, well-established companies.

You can (and should) request a **prospectus** for each fund you consider. The prospectus describes the fund in lengthy, boring language.

Mutual fund tables

Every Sunday when you were a kid, you would fight with your little brother or sister over the comics section, while your mom or dad hid behind those mystifying columns of numbers in the business section.

Unfortunately, after looking at these two pages, you'll discover that your parents weren't natural code-breakers.

Mutual fund and stock tables are actually easy to understand. Most papers carry the major funds and stocks every day in the business section.

Once you get your huge portfolio, you'll follow these tables more closely than Billy's footprints in "The Family Circus."

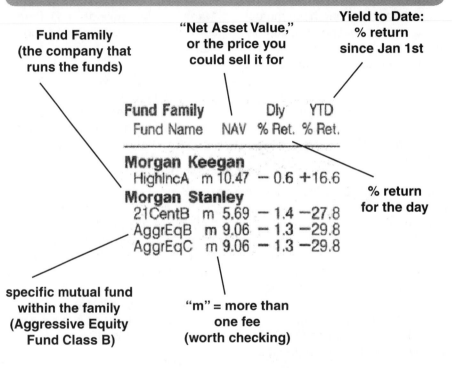

Fund Family (the company that runs the funds)

"Net Asset Value," or the price you could sell it for

Yield to Date: % return since Jan 1st

| Fund Family | | Dly | YTD |
Fund Name	NAV	% Ret.	% Ret.
Morgan Keegan			
HighIncA m	10.47	− 0.6	+16.6
Morgan Stanley			
21CentB m	5.69	− 1.4	−27.8
AggrEqB m	9.06	− 1.3	−29.8
AggrEqC m	9.06	− 1.3	−29.8

% return for the day

specific mutual fund within the family (Aggressive Equity Fund Class B)

"m" = more than one fee (worth checking)

Stock tables

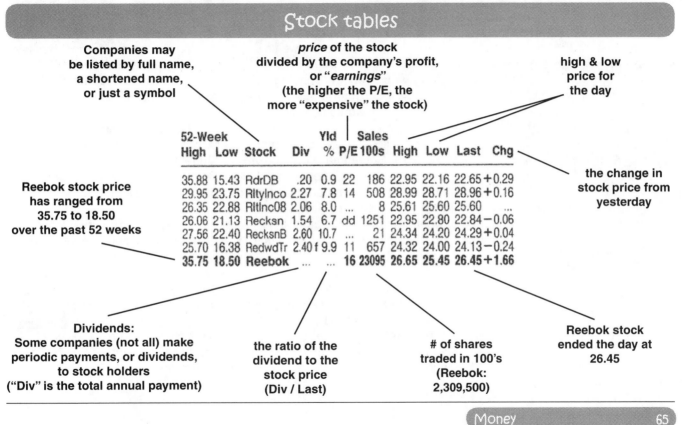

Companies may be listed by full name, a shortened name, or just a symbol

price of the stock divided by the company's profit, or "*earnings*" (the higher the P/E, the more "expensive" the stock)

high & low price for the day

52-Week		Stock	Div	Yld %	Sales				
High	Low	Stock	Div	% P/E	100s	High	Low	Last	Chg
35.88	15.43	RdrDB	.20	0.9 22	186	22.95	22.16	22.65	+0.29
29.95	23.75	RltyInco	2.27	7.8 14	508	28.99	28.71	28.96	+0.16
26.35	22.88	Rltlnc08	2.06	8.0 ...	8	25.61	25.60	25.60	...
26.06	21.13	Recksn	1.54	6.7 dd	1251	22.95	22.80	22.84	−0.06
27.56	22.40	RecksnB	2.60	10.7 ...	21	24.34	24.20	24.29	+0.04
25.70	16.38	RedwdTr	2.40 f	9.9 11	657	24.32	24.00	24.13	−0.24
35.75	**18.50**	**Reebok**	...	... 16	23095	26.65	25.45	26.45	+1.66

Reebok stock price has ranged from 35.75 to 18.50 over the past 52 weeks

the change in stock price from yesterday

Dividends: Some companies (not all) make periodic payments, or dividends, to stock holders ("Div" is the total annual payment)

the ratio of the dividend to the stock price (Div / Last)

# of shares traded in 100's (Reebok: 2,309,500)

Reebok stock ended the day at 26.45

"Giving it away" overview

So far, we've only been talking about "Bringing it in." Unfortunately, interest works both ways.

Just like love, interest comes and goes. Sometimes you receive it coming in; other times, you dole it out. Usually you end up giving more than you receive, but if you find the "right one," you'll end up getting more than you ever thought you could.

Before you know it, you'll have little interests running around your house. Just don't invite your interest-in-law to come live with you, or you could end up in an interesting fight.

When you use someone else's money, you have to pay for it. You pay interest. This is where "Giving it away" comes up.

The most common ways that people "Give it away" are through student loans and credit cards. Both charge you interest for using someone else's money.

Surprisingly, neither loans nor credit cards are inherently evil. Sometimes, giving your money away at a low rate can even be a *good* thing. If you use loans and credit cards properly, you'll certainly find more ways to *Love Your Money.*

Giving it away: Student loans

If George Orwell were around today, he might write, "All student loans are equal. But some are more equal than others." Or something like that.

Rates on student loans vary quite a bit based on the type of loan (Perkins, Stafford, Plus, etc.), school enrollment status, and the timing of when your loan started.

Since policy makers in Washington like to make life difficult for the authors of books covering the life skills needed after graduation, we can't include the giant matrix of current student loan rates. If you saw the grid, you'd hate us for even trying.

But, we'll tell you that rates are generally around 5% to 8%. If you're feeling crazy, **SallieMae.com** is a good source for more information. Rates reset on July 1st of every year (for new loans and loans that don't have fixed rates).

We'll also share with you some terms that you might find in your research:

Cap is the highest amount of interest you'll ever pay on your loan.

Grace Period describes the amount of time you have, after you graduate, before you have to start repaying your loan. In some cases, interest still accumulates during this time.

A number of secret perks exist that can save you some money on your student loans. This is the entrance to the Bat Cave. Are you ready, Robin?

Direct deposit
(Save 0.25%)

If you set up your loan account to have payments automatically withdrawn from your checking account each month, some lenders will give you 0.25% off your loan. Lenders feel a little security in having money automatically withdrawn for payments, so they cut you some slack. In this way, lenders are more beneficial than your tailor, who will only cut you some slacks.

If you have a loan charged at 5.25% interest, you'll only have to pay 5% with direct deposit. It doesn't sound like much, but it adds up -- just like those midnight runs to Taco Bell.

Timely payments
(Save 2%)

Some lenders who offer Stafford loans take 2% off your interest rate if you make your payments on time for four years.

Now you're only paying 3% interest on your loan. No, we will not shut up. These deals aren't available for everyone, but ask your lender.

Tax break
(Save something)

You can also get a tax break on the interest you pay on your student loans.

You can take a deduction of up to $2500 with no need to itemize (make a detailed list). This secret perk starts to disappear as soon as you make $50,000 a year and is gone at $65,000 ($100,000 to $130,000 for married folks).

If the sexy words "deduction" and "itemize" make you cringe, we de-mystify them for you in our chapter on taxes.

Subsidized loans

Subsidized loans are the best.

We talked earlier about the Rule of Money:

When you use someone else's money, you have to pay for it.

In this case, you get to break the rule. "Subsidized" means that the government pays your interest while you're in school. You get to use someone else's money (your lender's money) without paying interest.

If you're offered a subsidized loan and don't need the money, take the loan anyway and invest the money in a money market fund. You'll make some free money.

Repayment options

Most lenders give you a number of choices for paying off your loan.

Here are the most frequent repayment options:

Standard repayment
Payments are the same each month.

Graduated repayment
Payments start small and gradually increase.

Income-sensitive repayment
Payments are a percentage of your monthly income.

Extended repayment
Payments extend over 25 years (if eligible).

Consolidating

Consolidating means combining all of your student loans into one monthly payment and potentially lowering your interest rate (if rates are lower *now* than when you originally borrowed the money).

Contact your lender for details about consolidating. Also:

You have one shot. You can only consolidate *once*. If rates go lower, you can't consolidate again.

Utilize your grace period. In any given year, the rates on Stafford loans are lower during your grace period thanks to Uncle Sam. If you consolidate within your grace period of six months, you can *lock in* this lower rate. That's *Love!*

Giving it away:

Credit Cards

Credit cards are very demanding when it comes to interest. They usually charge around 18%, which is higher than almost any other type of loan.

Too many people carry large balances on their credit cards and only pay the minimum balance due on each statement.

If you manage to use your credit card wisely by paying off your balances and using a card with rewards, using a credit card can be one of the best ways to *Love Your Money*.

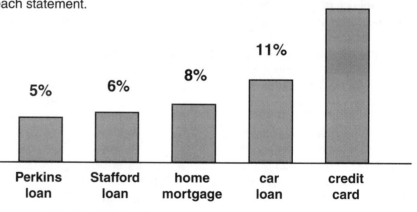

	Perkins loan	Stafford loan	home mortgage	car loan	credit card
	5%	6%	8%	11%	18%

Minimum payments on credit cards

Credit cards (or the banks that issue credit cards) make their money from your interest payments. The longer you take to pay back your balance, the more you pay in interest.

To encourage you to keep a balance on your card, cards offer you a low minimum payment on each bill.

If you had a balance of $4000, your minimum monthly payment would be only $83.33.

Q: If you <u>never</u> used your credit card again and only made the <u>minimum</u> payment each month, how long would it take you to pay off your balance?

The answer is below.

Account Summary									
	Previous Balance	(+)Purchases & Advances	(−)Payments	(−)Credits	(+)<u>Finance Charge</u>	(+)Late Charges	(=)New Balance	Purchases Minimum Due **83.33**
								Advances Minimum Due
								Amount Over Credit Line
Purchases Advances	1825.61	4183.99	2000.00	9.60			4000.00	Other ways to rip you off
								Past Due
Total	1825.61	4183.99	2000.00	9.60			4000.00	Minimum Amount Due (**83.33**)

Rate Summary	Purchases	Advances	
Number of days this Billing Period **31**			
Calculation Method	Daily	Daily	
Periodic Rate	.05041%	.05476%	
Nominal Annual Percentage Rate	18.400%	19.990%	
<u>Annual Percentage Rate</u>	18.400%	19.990%	
Balance Subject to Finance Charge			

A: Roughly **29 years and $13,000 later**, you'd pay off your balance. If you want to *Love* Your Money, pay the entire balance every month. (FYI: Minimum payments are usually the greater of $20 or 1/48th of the balance.)

Credit cards are often mentioned in the same breath as the devil's children. In reality, credit cards have no satanic lineage at all. In fact, to truly *Love Your Money,* you need to use credit cards religiously.

Credit cards have a number of fantastic perks:

Build your credit

Every time you buy something and pay it off quickly, the "credit police" put a gold star on your credit report (figuratively, of course). Your future landlord or bank lender likes to see those gold stars (literally).

A **credit report** is basically your financial transcript. Big Brother keeps track of all your financial dealings for the rest of the world to see. You can see an example of one on the next page.

If you ever want to see a copy of your credit report, you can order one on-line (for a small fee) at one of these sites:

Equifax	equifax.com
Experian	experian.com
Transunion	transunion.com

You're entitled to a free copy of your credit report within 60 days of rejection for credit, employment, insurance, or rental housing that was based upon your credit information (Fair Credit Reporting Act).

Free loan

When you purchase something with a credit card, you usually don't have to come up with the money for 15 to 30 days. If you pay your bill (in full) on time, you're not charged any interest. Remember the Rule:

**When you use
someone else's money,
you have to pay for it.**

Now *you're* not playing by the rules. You're borrowing someone else's money for 30 days and not paying for it.

Now *that's Love.*

Sample credit report

Personal Data

Louise Pindleberry
Branford, CT 06405

Social Security Number: 331-45-2121
Date of Birth: 2/19/75

Employment History

Happy Hospital

Location:
Erie, PA

Employment Date:
2/12/2005

Verified Date:
12/4/2008

Public Records

No bankruptcies on file.
No liens on file.

Credit Information

Company Name	Acct Number and Whose Acct	Date Opened	Last Activity	Type of Acct and Status	High Credit	Items as of Date Reported		Past Due	Date Reported
						Terms	Balance		
Capital Two	412654460 JOINT ACCT	02/99	12/08	Revolving PAYS AS AGREED	$800	16	$600		12/2008

they're
watching
you ...

Prior Paying History

30 days past due 03 times; 60 days past due 02 times; 90+ days past due 00 times
CREDIT CARD

Most importantly, credit cards come with rewards. Finally, someone appreciates your ability to spend money recklessly.

Credit card companies usually offer one of three types of rewards: money back, frequent flyer miles, and general points -- all better than the shiny nickels given to you by the old lady next door for giving daily washes between her toes.

Money back
You'll usually earn the equivalent of 1% of your purchases.

Frequent flyer miles
The value of these rewards varies based on the price of your ticket. Many domestic flights cost 25,000 miles. If your card pays you 1 point per mile (standard) and you use your rewards for a flight valued at greater than $250, then these points are worth *more than* 1% of your purchases.

General points
A few cards provide points good for any number of rewards (often worth roughly 1% of your purchases as well).

Many of these rewards cards charge an annual fee. If you spend more than $5000 a year on a card with an annual fee of $50, the value of your rewards will outweigh the cost of the fee. If you spend a lot, *get yourself a card with rewards.*

Your parents always answered questions with "It depends." "Can I spend the night at Bert's?" "Do you love me more than the cat?"

The question of "Which card is best for me?" also has to be answered with "It depends."

If you fly a lot, you should look into getting a card with frequent flier miles, because they can be worth *more* than 1% of your purchases. If you fly one airline more than others, look on that airline's website for card offers.

But if you spend a lot, *get yourself a card with rewards.*

Big, dramatic conclusion

If you're a human being (our target audience), you spend money.

If you could get rewarded for charging the money you normally spend, why wouldn't you?

If you want to *Love Your Money:*

Get a credit card that pays you rewards.

Get rid of those boring credit cards that do nothing for you.

Credit card companies charge merchants every time a credit card purchase is made in a store. If your bill is $10, the store only gets $9.70 of that. The credit card company gets the other $0.30. If the credit card company is willing to share some of its loot with you, why not take it?

Once you get a card with rewards:

Use your card for *all* of your *normal* purchases.

Don't buy an unneeded pair of shoes simply because you want to rack up frequent flier miles. Rather, *every time* you buy groceries, movie tickets, gas, or anything you *normally* would purchase with cash, **use your credit card with rewards.**

If you don't get squat for using cash or check, why ever use them?

Debit Cards

If you don't have any self-control with a credit card, then get a **debit card with rewards**.

A debit card works the same way as a check. When your card is swiped, money is automatically withdrawn from your account. Once your bank account runs dry, your debit card doesn't work anymore.

A few debit cards with rewards exist, but they usually pay half as well as credit cards. That being said, they're still better than cash.

Here's one additional drawback to consider: Rental car companies will not accept a debit card to hold a car. You may not have any cash in your account to pay for their car when you drive it into a tree.

Giving it away:

Mortgages

Mortgages overview

A home is different from almost anything else you'll ever buy.

First off, you may only have to pony up $15,000 for a $150,000 home. You can borrow the rest.

Can you see yourself walking into a department store, smacking down $15 for a $150 sweater, and saying, "Don't worry, I'll just borrow the rest"?

Second, you'll have a gajillion different ways to borrow the rest.

Can you see someone in the department store running up to you and yelling: "Hey, you can borrow the rest from me! Would you like an ARM, a balloon, or an IO?" Uh... what?

Third, you can usually resell your home for more than you paid for it.

Can you see trying to resell your $150 sweater five years later for $200? Good luck. Try Goodwill.

Figuring out the finances on a home purchase can be confusing, but the choices you make here count a lot more than the size of your fries and soda. We'll help you ask the right questions.

So what's a mortgage? Technically speaking, it's someone's right to your home if you don't make your payments. But technically speaking, that's really boring.

So what's a **mortgage**? For the rest of us, a mortgage is a fancy word for the loan you need to buy your home. If you can pay $15,000 for a $150,000 home, you'll need a $135,000 mortgage to make up the difference. Below are some words you'll see.

The **term,** or length, of a mortgage can vary. It's usually 15 or 30 years long (though you won't necessarily keep it that long). If mortgages were shorter, like 5 years, your monthly payments would be much, much larger.

Your **down payment** is the money that comes out of your pocket to pay for your home. This can be anywhere from 0% to over 20% of your purchase price.

We previously learned in the chapter that when you use some else's money, you have to pay for it. You'll pay interest here, too.

The interest rate and fees for your mortgage will vary from lender to lender, so it's a good idea to shop around. Visit local banks, contact a mortgage broker, or compare rates on websites like Bankrate.com.

When comparing interest rates, be sure to compare the **APR**, or annual percentage rate. This rate will include all fees charged by your lender, allowing you to fairly compare different offers.

Once you finally reach your **closing** (when you sign your papers), you'll have to pay a variety of **closing costs**.

Closing costs come in a variety of shapes and colors. You may encounter points, discount points, application fees, credit report fees, appraisal fees, inspection fees, and so on. Most of these will be due at your closing (on top of your down payment – yippee!). Your real estate agent will provide you a list of all of these costs before closing.

You'll have a choice between a few different types of mortgages. Your choice will determine how your monthly payment is calculated.

Fixed-rate mortgages: Your monthly payment stays the same every single month. Even if mortgage rates go up or down, your payment stays the same.

But, if rates drop a whole lot, you can **refinance,** which means that you can go to your lender and say: "Yuck! My rate is too high! I'd like to call a 'do-over' and get the new, lower rate." You'll have to pay some fees to do this, but if the current rate is low enough, refinancing may be worth it for you.

Adjustable-rate mortgages

(ARMs): Your payment will go up or down based on current interest rates.

You may hear of a 5/1 ARM or 10/1 ARM. This means that your rate is fixed for 5 or 10 years, but then adjusts up or down every 1 year after that.

ARMs are a little bit of a gamble. If you know that you'll be moving in five or ten years, then you'll be finished with your mortgage before it resets to a higher rate. But if you stay in your house for twenty years, you may find yourself making a much higher payment each month.

When you're applying for your mortgage, ask for "an ARM and a leg," with a goofy smile – we *guarantee* that your lender will think you're the funniest person alive.

Oh-Shoot!-I-Can't-Afford-My-Payments-Anymore mortgages (OSICAMPAMs): You may encounter a few crazy options that involve low initial payments that turn into much larger payments as time goes on (interest-only loans, balloons, and so on). Some of these can burn you over time, so make sure you understand all the terms of your mortgage before you sign on the dotted line.

One of the hardest things about buying a home is saving enough money for the down payment.

Why is a down payment so important? Suppose you borrowed $135,000 to buy a $150,000 home. Then suppose you ran off to a small village in Ecuador never to be heard from again. Your lender would be upset. Your mother would be furious.

Your lender would want his money back. If he sold your house for only $140,000, he would still get all of his money back because of the "cushion" of your $15,000 down payment. But your mother would still be furious.

Therefore, most lenders require that you make a down payment of at least 20%. If that's too steep, you'll probably have to purchase **mortgage insurance.** This can go by a number of different names (none of which we'd recommend as a name for your first child): PMI, MIP, and MMI.

By purchasing mortgage insurance, you may be allowed to put down as little as 5% of the purchase price. Plus, this fee can usually be included in your monthly mortgage payments.

If a 5% down payment is still too much, you many want to look into getting a **government-backed** mortgage from the **FHA** (Federal Housing Authority).

Why would the government help *you* out? Did he see what you did Friday night? Well, Uncle Sam likes to promote home ownership.

You'll still have to pay for mortgage insurance, but an FHA loan allows you to purchase a home with as little as 3% down, and the interest rate can be lower than traditional mortgages.

FHA sets some standards for your house, neighborhood, and credit quality to determine if you're cool enough to qualify to sit at his lunch table.

Ask your broker about your options. Now you'll be armed with questions to ask.

Equity

Since you're reading this, you're probably interested in buying instead of renting a place. Why do so many people buy? There are many reasons, but one of the biggest is usually financial. When deciding, you should consider three things:

One, home prices often go up — no one's making any more land.

Two, part of your mortgage payments are tax deductible, unlike rent. Uncle Sam helps you out.

Three, when you make mortgage payments, some of your payment goes toward paying off your house. When you rent, you'll never see that money again (unless you're dating your landlord, but whatever).

This brings us to one of your favorite words (or one that soon will be): **Equity** is what's yours.

If you put $15,000 "down" to purchase a $150,000 home, $15,000 is yours. You have $15,000 in equity. Although you own the whole house, the rest of it isn't really "yours." If you sold your home tomorrow, you'd have to pay back the $135,000.

But here's the cool part: If the value of your home goes up by $5,000 (values frequently go up), *all* of this **appreciation** is yours.

In fact, percentage-wise, this appreciation can often be pretty significant. If you initially put down $15,000 and you make $5,000, your equity has appreciated by 33%. Ka-ching.

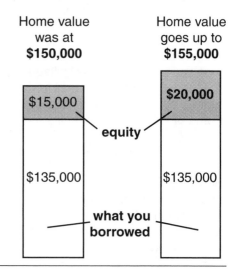

Home value was at **$150,000**   Home value goes up to **$155,000**

$15,000 $20,000

equity

$135,000 $135,000

what you borrowed

Now that you know about mortgages and equity, let's talk about your **mortgage payments**. You should know where your money is going.

Let's say you borrow $135,000 over 30 years at a fixed rate of 6%. (Did you ever think you'd read a sentence like that and *keep reading*? Well, buckle your seatbelt!)

Your mortgage payment will probably be due every month. When you make your payment, some of your money will be used to pay interest (remember: when you use someone else's money, you have to pay for it) and the rest will be used to pay off what you borrowed (the $135,000, or the **principal**).

The chart below is interesting (well, *sort of* interesting). In the first few years, the majority of each payment is used to pay interest.

For example, in year one, you'll pay close to $8,000 of your $10,000 in payments for interest. The rest of your payment will pay down your principal (which becomes your

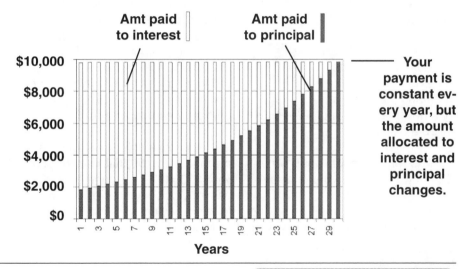

Amt paid to interest

Amt paid to principal

Years

Your payment is constant every year, but the amount allocated to interest and principal changes.

equity). But as time goes by, more and more of your payments will go toward paying off your principal.

Why? Well, at the beginning of your loan, you're paying interest on $135,000 (your whole loan). If you multiply this number by your 6% interest rate, you'll get about $8,000 (if you get a different number, remember to carry the three and the two – or try a new machine called a *calculator*).

The remainder of your payment ($2,000) pays down your principal.

But in year two, you'll be paying interest on *less* principal (since you paid $2,000 of it off in year one). So, more of your $10,000 yearly payment will go toward principal instead of interest.

How did we decide on the yearly payment number of $10,000? In our example, it's the number that results in a $0 balance on your mortgage after 30 years. Search the internet for "mortgage calculator" to try this yourself. (Note: The first time you search for this, you'll officially become an adult.)

In our example, you'll end up paying over **$150,000** in interest on your $135,000 mortgage over 30 years. Ouch! But there is a way to avoid paying so much interest (besides fleeing to Ecuador).

If you can afford it, consider **prepaying** some of your mortgage.

If you pay an extra $100 each month on your payment, that $100 immediately reduces your principal amount. This money not only adds to your equity, but it makes your *future* payments more significant.

Why? Since your principal is smaller, your future *interest* payments are smaller. Your total payment due stays the same each month, but more of your future payments will go toward paying down your principal rather than paying all that interest.

If you prepay every month, your thirty-year mortgage will be a lot shorter than thirty years.

Giving it away:

Bad Credit

There's no magical cure for bad credit. **Credit problems stay on your record for seven years** (ten years for bankruptcies). Try to start fixing your problems now.

Consolidate to low rates

Put all of your balances on one card with a low interest rate. Many cards offer a low (temporary) introductory **teaser rate** as an incentive to move your balance. Take them up on their offer, and save yourself some money in interest payments.

Consolidating your credit debt into one account prevents you from making further purchases, because you have a smaller remaining credit line. Plus, the credit police like to see that you have fewer spending opportunities. One monthly payment also simplifies your bill paying.

Make a plan

Again, there's no magic plan to solving credit problems. Sit down and lay out all of your income and expenses. Give yourself a budget that will afford you the opportunity to pay off your balances.

In one of our seminars, a student asked, "Hypothetically speaking, what if my *friend* bought a car on his credit card and doesn't have the money to pay for it?"

Our Guide replied, "Your *friend* should get a hypothetical job."

The easiest way to fix your credit problems is to avoid getting into them in the first place. This might be easier said then done, but we won't be able to sleep at night unless we tell you these obvious (or not so obvious) tips.

Live within your paycheck. No, duh. But when you pass that window with those brown alligator skin Manolo Blahniks staring up at you with a $2500 price tag, how can you resist? Only $1250 a shoe!

Even if you're not a Carrie Bradshaw wannabe, a plane ticket, rent, or a dinner out can break the budget. To *Love* your money, you'll need to live within your paycheck.

As soon as you start leaving balances on your credit card, you not only pay interest *now*, but you have less money to buy stuff *later*. And before you know it, later will become now and you'll be itching to buy more stuff with less money.

Beware of "the monthly." Many high ticket items (cars, electronics, etc.) are pitched by their low monthly costs. What sounds like the better deal?

(a) $399 per month
(b) $10,000 now

Based on the above, the answer is "Who knows?" How many months will you be paying?

When you purchase something on a monthly basis, **you're buying it on credit**. In the fine print, you'll find your interest rate.

If you pay $399 for 36 months, you'll end up paying over $14,000. The extra $4,000 you pay over three years is the cost for paying over time (interest). Do the fancy math (monthly payment x months) and *then* make your decision.

Living on credit is like carrying around a leaky bucket. As water (interest) keeps leaking out of your bucket (savings), you'll have less and less to spend down the road. That's certainly not *Love*.

Uniting the Love

After describing "Bringing it in" and "Giving it away," this section puts it all together. This is where everything falls into place and you get a warm fuzzy.

At the beginning of the chapter, we mentioned the idea that the interest you *pay* is the same as the interest you *earn*.

At some point, you should look at all the places where you're *earning* interest and all the places where you're *paying* interest. Then take a look at all of the different interest rates.

Compare your credit card and loan rates to your savings account and money market fund rates. Where is most of your money?

What interest rates are you paying and receiving?

You should move your money to the *highest* interest rate.

If your credit card charges you **18%**, but you earn **5%** on your money market fund, put most of your money towards your credit card. A rate of **18%** is certainly the highest.

If your car loan charges you **2%**, but you earn **5%** on your money market fund, put most of your money in your money market fund. The **5%** rate is higher.

The next two examples should make this clear. This is how to *Love Your Money*.

Example 1

If you have a balance on your credit card, you should obviously try to pay off your debt as soon as possible. An 18% rate is obnoxious.

At the same time, you should look at your investments. If you have money in a money market fund paying you 5%, you should *take money out of this account to pay off your card.* Keep a reserve, but do this to save yourself money.

If you're paying 18% to earn 5%, you're losing money, when you could be paying off your credit card bill more quickly.

Example 2

Imagine that you have a special rate on a car loan where you only pay 2% interest. If you have the opportunity to pay off that loan early, you should resist the temptation. Keep your money with the highest interest rate.

Keep your loan for as long as you can, because your loan has a low rate. You are making money by borrowing at a low rate and investing at a high rate.

The same holds true for low-interest student loans. Keep them. If you can borrow at a low rate and invest at a higher rate, you can make a little extra money for yourself. That's *Love*!

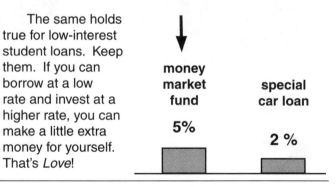

Seminar Three

Getting Your Apartment

Jenny proved too immature to be a realtor.

Getting Your Apartment

As you probably expect, getting an apartment varies tremendously from city to city.

In this chapter, we'll explain some universal truths that you'll need to know for apartment shopping in virtually any city. We run through tips for:

- **Before you get there**
- **Once you're in the city**
- **Closing the deal**
- **Signing the lease**

As Bert's senior year was winding down, he took the role of a "casual observer" in his preparation for finding an apartment. In other words, he didn't do anything.

Bert planned on staying on a friend's couch for a few days, opening up the newspaper, and finding an ad that read:

> ```
> Huge one bdrm.  $500/mo.
> Only renting to people
> named Bert.
> ```

Six months and three couches later, Bert finally found a place he could call home.

This chapter will help you avoid some of Bert's pitfalls. Not only will it help you find an apartment, but it will help you find a place that *you'll like for the next few years.* Anyone can find an overpriced, tiny apartment in a bad area of town. We'll help you find a place you can be proud to call your own.

Before you get there

Web resources

The web has a few good sites that can help you before your move. Our favorite is a site put out by the US Postal Service:

www.MoversGuide.com

In stark contrast to many government agencies, the site is comprehensive and efficient. It will give you an idea of what you should think about prior to your move (packing, change of address, etc.).

Two of the biggest national apartment search websites are:

www.Apartments.com
www.Move.com

These sites are broad in scope, with numerous listings.

Spread the word

One of the most important things you can do prior to your move is **tell people that you're looking for an apartment.**

Tell anyone and everyone you know. You'd be amazed at how many apartments never make it onto the rental market.

You'll never know if your best friend's sister's boyfriend's brother's girlfriend will know this one guy who knows this one kid ... who might be renting out an apartment in Tulsa next month.

Tell everyone. You never know.

Roommates

You may be looking forward to finally living on your own, but a roommate can significantly cut the price you pay in rent.

Why? The bathroom and the kitchen are the most expensive rooms in an apartment. The fixtures, appliances, and plumbing are expensive for your landlord to buy and maintain. When you have a roommate, you're essentially splitting these costs (unless you each have your own bathroom and kitchen, of course).

Also, don't underestimate the value of a roommate for security and social reasons, especially if you're moving to a city.

Credit issues

When you finally find an apartment, your landlord will check your credit before he or she gives you the keys.

Believe it or not, every single credit card bill and loan payment you ever made is recorded by a credit agency. Your landlord will check to see if you pay your bills. If you have bad credit, you'll have the adult equivalent of Cooties.

If you're curious about your credit status, you can order a report (for a small fee) through these sites:

Equifax	equifax.com
Experian	experian.com
Transunion	transunion.com

Also, no credit is bad credit. Not having credit is like not having your Cooties vaccine.

Never having used a credit card doesn't help your situation much either. A Nebraska farm boy we'll call Bailey was turned down for an apartment in NYC because he had never used a credit card. His credit wasn't bad, but he couldn't prove that he paid his bills on time.

We talk about suggestions for fixing your bad credit in our "Love Your Money" chapter.

Once you've got your credit report in order, start saving some money.

Depending on what city you'll be moving to, you may need a lot of money up front to get a place.

Most new apartments require at least one month's rent up front. Others can require the first month, the last month, a security deposit (the equivalent of a month), and a broker's fee. This works out to:

four months rent up front.

Four months is the rare exception, but most book writers like to include the extreme cases of some things to make the text more dramatic!!

We called home after we got our first apartments and talked to Mom. "The good news is I got a place. The bad news is I spent all my cash. I'm broke and hungry." Moms love phone calls like that.

If you're already broke, try to work out a deal with your parents to spot you some money for a little while.

When you go to sign your lease, your landlord likely won't accept an out-of-state check for your deposit. He or she will require a **cash equivalent**, like a money order or cashier's check.

These two items are considered "cash equivalents" because they can't bounce. You need to have money in your account for a bank to issue you a cash equivalent. The bank will hold this money in your account until your money order or cashier's check clears.

When the time comes to pay for your apartment, you could arrive with a briefcase full of twenties in the trunk of your Buick (plus a crowbar, in case you need to "persuade" the super to keep the rent fair). Alternatively, set up an account in a bank that has a branch in your new city. Then you can get a cashier's check. Set up your account early: your bank may require a week's wait before you can write checks.

Once you're in the city

Small audiences

When shopping for an apartment, look at advertisements with **small audiences**, rather than at large newspaper listings.

Smaller newspapers, apartment listings within your work, local laundromats, fliers on telephone polls, and alumni groups will offer places with less competition. You'll often find places with more "character" in these listings, instead of large apartment complexes.

Additionally, people like to rent to others who have some commonality, such as the same school or workplace. You might come across a good deal this way.

Personal ads

Once you've tried the small audiences, you'll have to scour the large newspaper listings.

Finding a good apartment from a classified ad can be difficult. Much like the personal ads, you'll need to "read between lines" to decipher the ad's true meaning.

Is this bachelor a catch?

```
SM, 39, ISO S/DF, 25-
35, for laughter and
companionship. Enjoys
sports, music, dinner
with friends. Looking
for motivated woman. No
material girls.
```

Personal ads (cont.)

This single male in search of a single or divorced female may sound like a winner, but before you pick up the phone, let's translate what the ad is *really* trying to say.

A single male at age 39? Serious commitment issues.

Sports, music, dinner with friends? Or should that read: "Gambling, drinking, and smoking"?

SM, 39, ISO S/DF, 25-35, for laughter and companionship. Enjoys sports, music, dinner with friends. Looking for motivated woman. No material girls.

He doesn't want any material girls? Ladies, you know what this means. He's broke, unemployed, and still living in the basement.

Newspaper ads

The same thing holds true for apartment ads. You need to read between the lines. For example:

"Cozy" is another word for "no room for a bed."

Lovely, cozy studio. Only 10-minutes to sub-way. Up-and-coming neighborhood. $650/mo.

"Up-and-coming neighborhood" really means *not good right now.*

Apartment lingo

Now that you have your radar up for deceptive ads, here is some lingo you should know.

Walk-up
No elevator

Duplex
Two-level unit

Alcove
Partly enclosed area connected to a room

Studio
One room or one room connected to a kitchen

Junior one-bedroom
Tiny room off the living room which may only fit a bed

Abbrev.

As you're looking at ads, you'll quickly be amazed at the liberties taken with the English language. You may confuse many of the ads with a word scramble puzzle. These are some common abbreviations:

h/w
Hardwood floors

DW
Dishwasher

EIK
Eat-in kitchen

WIC
Walk-in closet

W/D
Washer and dryer

Brokers

In some cities, you'll *have* to use a broker. In other spots, they don't even exist. Brokers basically own the market in some bigger cities.

At the same time, brokers can serve as a great resource. They may turn out to be your best friend … because brokers' hearts are just so darn big – or because they get paid handsome commissions.

Always lowball your price.
If you can only pay $800, tell the broker you can only pay $600.

No matter what kind of apartment you need, you're going to hear the same thing: "Wow, I don't have

Brokers (Cont.)

a lot of listings in that price range, but I do have apartments for $200 more."

You'll say, "That's convenient, because I was hoping not to have any money for food and *silly* little things like that."

Think of this as a game of poker. If you show your broker your cards right away, he or she is going to raise you until you're broke.

Do not put your full faith in one broker. Use many. You're going to pay one a lot of money. Make them work a little bit for your cash.

Don't feel bad saying no 100 times. They're used to it.

Things to check

When you're looking at places, *make a list* of things to check. Once you move in, you'll enjoy those "trivial" extras like *running* water and a toilet *that flushes*. Remember to check:

light switches	elevator
air conditioner	heat
appliances	noise level
hot water	windows
leaks under sink	damages
proximity to subway	parking

After you've looked at the place with a broker, pull this sneaky little trick. **Tell your broker that you forgot your coat** (purse, dentures, whatever) **in the apartment.** Go back "to get it" while your broker waits for you *outside*.

Once you return to the apartment, ask the current tenant or a neighbor a few questions. You'll get your first unbiased, honest answers all day. Is the apartment loud? Does the super (superintendent) own a wrench?

It might be best to keep looking if you hear, "I don't mind the bugs – they usually keep to themselves."

If you have time, walk around the neighborhood to make sure you feel safe. Try to visit the neighborhood in the day *and* at night. The night crowd is often dramatically different from the day crowd.

Closing the deal

Things to bring

In many big cities, you'll need to act quickly once you've found your place. In some competitive cities, if you see a place you like, you take it on the spot. There's nothing worse than finding a place you really like, only to have it ripped away by someone who moved faster than you did.

Make sure you have:

money orders / cash equivalents
driver's license
references
credit report
(you may save money
if you get the report yourself)

Have your previous landlord fill out this sample reference letter:

Sample letter

Dear _____,

It is with pleasure that I write this letter of recommendation for [name]. When [name] vacated his/her apartment unit, it was in better condition than when he/she moved into it.

During his/her [number]-year residency at [Cap & Compass Apartments], [name] has been an excellent member of our rental community.

Whenever it snowed, he/she made hot cocoa for all the children and purchased groceries for our older residents.

I will surely miss the smell of [name]'s apple pies filling the hallways and the way he/she sang with the robin on sunny mornings.

I am not a spiritual person by nature, but I do believe that if angels live among us, [name] surely walks among them.

Sincerely,

Property Manager
[Cap & Compass Apartments]

Signing the lease

The problem with leases is that they are large documents written in small print using big words. The authors try to discourage people from actually reading them. Take this excerpt from a lease:

> ENTIRE AGREEMENT: This agreement contains the entire agreement between parties hereto and neither party is bound by any representations or agreements of any kind except as contained herein.

Translation:

This is your lease.

This being said, make sure you read your lease. These are the things to look for:

Make sure the *length* of the lease is expressly written in the contract. Do not accept a month-to-month contract, or you could get booted.

Determine who is responsible for fixing appliances. Some landlords are only responsible for repairing *permanent* fixtures, such as the sink, shower, and toilet. If that's the case, make sure you're handy with a wrench or have the survival skills to keep your food cold in the toilet.

Confirm that your apartment will be cleaned (and assessed for damage) prior to your arrival. If the floors are warped and the landlord doesn't know about it until you move out, your security deposit pays for it.

Confirm that your security deposit is going into an inter-est- bearing account. Most state laws mandate this. When you get your deposit back, you should get back more than you gave – assuming they don't charge you for those warped floor boards.

Determine your future rent increases. Some states (New York, Maryland, California, New Jersey, and DC) have rent control laws. You never want to be surprised by a massive rent hike once you have all of your stuff on the walls and don't feel like moving.

Make sure your privacy rights are spelled out. Most states require landlords to provide advance notice (usually 24 hours) when they are going to enter your apartment (unless it's an emergency). No one likes Billy Bob fixing their sink while they're in the shower. The only thing worse is when you've just gotten out of the shower and you're caught dancing naked for your plants to old Michael Jackson songs (hypothetically speaking, of course).

Finally, and most importantly, **make sure you have everything in writing.** You don't want to get involved in a he-said, she-said argument when your landlord doubles your rent. If everything is in writing, you'll have a case.

If you're moving to a new location, be sure to check out our city-specific **starter kits**.

These handy guides provide local insight into the apartment market, provide needed paperwork (auto registration, voter ID, etc.), help with setting up utilities, and much more.

You can learn about our starter kits on our website at:

www.CapandCompass.com

The list of cities (such as LA, NYC, Boston, San Fran, and many more) is growing every day, so please check back if your city isn't listed.

Seminar Four

W4401kHMO: Translating Day 1 at Work

No one followed Chuck's lead to initiate
Risky Business casual.

W4401KHMO: Translating Day 1 at Work

Your first day on the job isn't that different from your first day of kinder-garten, except that everyone shaves and Milk Time has been replaced with Happy Hour.

In kindergarten, you're sup-posed to show up at 9 a.m. and wear something nice. You're going to learn a bunch of new things about "school" and you have no idea where to sit at lunch.

The same thing goes for work. You show up at 9 a.m. and wear something nice. You're going to learn a bunch of new things about "work" and you still don't know where to sit at lunch.

In this chapter, we'll explain:

- **Work attire**
- **HMOs & PPOs**
- **401k's**
- **That tax form (the W-4)**
- **Work etiquette**

Your decisions on the first day won't be that difficult, but you prob-ably haven't had to deal with many of them before now. This chapter will help you make smart choices.

Unfortunately, when it comes to where to sit at lunchtime, you're on your own. If you're a dork, you're probably out of luck.

Work attire

Back in junior high school, you used to look good in your Doc Martens and "Yo quiero Taco Bell" t-shirt. The appropriate dress code for work is often just as peculiar.

The attire at most workplaces can be classified into one of two categories. If you scored yourself a plum job with a large company, you may have to dress:

business professional.

Clients might visit the office at any moment, so you'll need to look smooth.

If your office goes casual on Fridays or if you found yourself a paycheck in a less formal environment, you may be allowed to dress:

business casual.

If you're capable of getting a job, you're probably capable of dressing for work. However, there are a couple of things that you should keep in mind as you prepare for day one in the workforce.

In this section, we'll give some tips for both men and women for "business professional" and "business casual." Throw in an apple for your boss and a little common sense, and you should be fine on your big first day.

Work attire:

Business profess-ional

Business suits

Buy wool. Wool suits last longer, breathe better, and wrinkle less than any other type of suit.

If you have to wear suits, buy at least two and keep them basic. You may think you look good in the olive green, but after a few weeks you'll be known as "Olive Green Suit Boy."

At lunch, your co-workers will huddle up at their table and cackle, "Did you see Olive Green Suit Boy today? Today he's wearing a *blue* tie ... like that makes it a new outfit."

They're not laughing *with* you, they're laughing *at* you. Blue and gray suits might seem boring, but boring doesn't get noticed or ridiculed.

Shirts

You'll want at least seven shirts. We know shirts aren't cheap, but if you have fewer than seven shirts, you'll visit your dry cleaner so often that he'll think you're sweet on him.

Expect to pay $1.50 for each shirt to be dry-cleaned. You can resort to the ol' washer and dryer to save yourself a few bucks, but prepare to become an ironing expert.

Stiffners

Dress shirts usually come in two main styles: the traditional **button-down** with button holes on the collar and the **spread-style** with no buttons.

Spread-style collars come with

Men (cont.)

something called **collar stays** or **collar stiffners**.

These are used to keep your collar from curling up and they usually come with the shirt. Remember

they fit in a little pocket in your collar

to *take them out when you wash your shirt*. Otherwise, you'll have collar stay marks that never go away.

Business professional for women

Hanger rule
Women, when dressing business professional, remember to abide by the **hanger rule.**

The "hanger rule" states that you need to:

Buy your entire outfit off one hanger.

In other words, you're not allowed to mix and match a skirt or pants with a jacket from a different outfit. If you purchased your jacket and pants on the same hanger, then you're safe in a business professional environment.

Other rules
Stay away from open-toed shoes, too much perfume, high-heels (medium to flat is ok), sleeveless tops, dangling bracelets, more than one necklace, or anything too revealing. Men, all of these rules go for you, too.

Stick with black, gray, dark burgundy, or navy suits with simple lines and no ruffles or pleats. Find something that you can wear with confidence.

Basically, if you think that you could go out dancing right after work without changing your clothes, you probably want to rethink your outfit.

Work attire: Business Casual

Every company has a different definition of business casual. Some require suits (sans the tie) while others permit flip-flops. There are no hard and fast rules for business casual, but below are some things to remember:

Always overdress for the first day of work. Look at your colleagues on the first day and decide how casual you can be for Day Two.

There is one exception to this rule: rodeo clowns. If you're entering this field, you probably already have the whole "work outfit" thing figured out. If that's the case, good luck and make sure you *stretch*.

Buy the majority of your wardrobe *after* your first day of work. Wait to see what the cool cats around the office are wearing these days. Then you'll own work clothes that you *actually want to wear to work*.

Even the phrase "business casual" still has the word "business" in it. This means **you should stay dressy**: tuck shirts in, don't reveal too much skin, and always iron your clothes.

 No one likes to iron, but looking like a slob is unacceptable at work. Your friends expect you to look like a slob. They know you're a slob. They like you as a slob. But the workplace is a different story.

Health insurance

Now you've got your favorite new threads and you're ready to head out the door. If you're working for a large company, your human resources manager will be waiting for you.

He or she will give you all sorts of exciting paperwork to fill out, beginning with **health insurance**.

Up until now, you've probably been covered by your parents' insurance plan. Once you graduate, you'll need your own policy. In fact, many states kick you off your parents' insurance plan when you turn 23 or are no longer a full-time student.

Health insurance is an important benefit. If you *don't* have health insurance, something as minor as a broken arm could set you back thousands of dollars. A more serious condition could put a drain on your bank account for years.

This section will give you a *general* overview of health insurance and the different plans available to you. The variations on each plan are nearly infinite. The difference between some HMOs and PPOs becomes one giant blur.

When you sit down to get insurance, *take the time to read over your plan in detail.* Speak to your insurance agent (if you have one) and ask a lot of questions.

Overview (Cont.)

The decisions you make now about insurance coverage are important because you're usually only allowed to change your plan once a year.

You can't get sick and then say, "Ooh, ooh! I want the good plan now." They've figured that one out already.

Your employer will probably offer you its most cost-effective option. Occasionally, you may be allowed to upgrade your plan if you kick in some money of your own.

We'll walk through your different options and explain the standard plans. Before we do, here are some of the words that you'll encounter in virtually every plan.

Insurance Jargon

Most plans talk the same jive:

Deductible
The dollar amount (usually per calendar year) you need to pay for medical expenses before the insurance kicks in.

Co-payment
A small fee (often $5 to $20) you pay every time you visit a doctor.

Premium
Your monthly payment for insurance coverage. Your employer may pay some of your premium.

PCP
A Primary Care Physician: the family doctor you often need to contact before you can see a specialist. Often referred to as a "gatekeeper."

Out-of-pocket maximum
The most money you'll have to pay in a calendar year for "reasonable" and "customary" care. Your insurance will pick up the costs above this amount.

Payable in Pop-Tarts
If you see this expression in an insurance document, it is a telltale sign that something is wrong. Use caution if your insurance agent weaves this into the conversation.

Pre-existing condition
This requirement to disclose your allergy to whale blubber can actually help you when you end up in an emergency room and the doctors contact your insurer for information about your medical history.

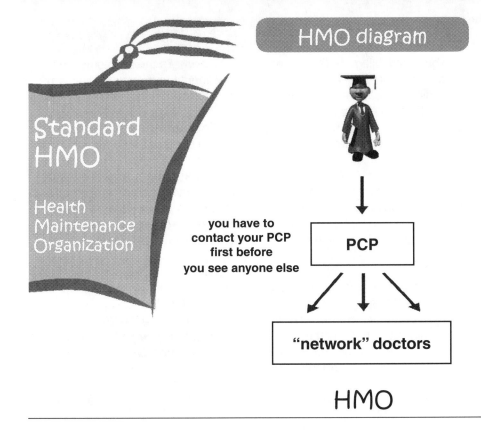

you have to contact your PCP first before you see anyone else

PCP

"network" doctors

HMO

Standard HMO

Health Maintenance Organization

To your left is your basic health plan, the standard **HMO**. Of the plans we cover, it's usually the least expensive and the least flexible.

When you sign up with an HMO, your insurance company will provide you a **phone book** of doctors approved by the plan. These are called your **in-network doctors**. If you visit any doctors *outside* of this network, you're on your own when paying the bill (except for emergencies).

Imagine you are a mermaid and you want to remove your tail. Or more realistically, pretend for a moment that you are afflicted with "Too Many Fingers." For our readers with eleven or twelve places for your school ring, we sympathize with your awkward condition. We know elementary school was tough, so we'll cover this quickly.

Let's suppose you have six fingers on your left hand. Your local drugstore doesn't carry finger removal cream, so you need to see a specialist.

If you were part of an HMO, the best finger removal specialist in the country, Dr. Fingerbegone, might not be in your network, or phone book. In order for your insurance company to pick up some of the cost, you might have to use a local specialist (Dr. Chopitov) who has only removed a "handful" of unwanted fingers.

You could still go to Dr. Finger-begone, but you'd have to pay the *entire* bill yourself. For this reason, a network is often unpopular since you're restricted as to what doctors you can visit under the plan.

The standard HMO has another restriction. Within this phone book of doctors, you're required to pick *one* as your main doctor (usually a family doctor). We'll call this doctor "Dr. Friendly."

Dr. Friendly is your **PCP**, or **Primary Care Physician**. If you get sick, you go to Dr. Friendly first. If you sprain your ankle, you go to Dr. Friendly. If you get a pencil stuck in your ear, you see Dr. Friendly.

So what's the problem? When Dr. Friendly gives you a shot, you get a lollipop, right?

The problem is that you *always* have to contact Dr. Friendly before you can see Dr. Skin, Dr. Nose, or Dr. Fingerbegone. *Your insurance will not cover visits to any other doctors unless you have a **referral** from Dr. Friendly* (there are a few exceptions, like emergencies).

Once again, this isn't very flexible. Now consider the case of the standard PPO.

Standard HMO Summary
Less expensive, less flexible.
Must contact your
PCP every time.
Must stay in-network.

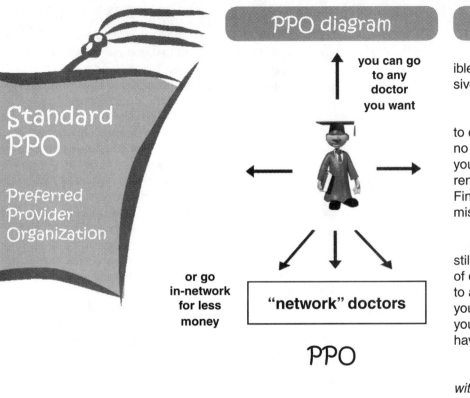

you can go to any doctor you want

or go in-network for less money

"network" doctors

PPO

A **PPO** is often your most flexible plan, but also the most expensive.

Under a PPO, you don't have to choose one main doctor (there's no Dr. Friendly). This means that if you need to get an unwanted finger removed, you can go directly to Dr. Fingerbegone without getting permission from anyone else.

Your insurance company will still provide you with a phone book of doctors. But this time, if you go to a doctor *outside* the phone book, your insurance company will help you pay for some of the bill. You'll have more flexibility.

Of course, if you choose from *within* your phone book, you'll pay

Standard PPO

Preferred Provider Organization

Explanation (cont.)

less of the bill, but at least your insurance company will pay for some of the costs for **out-of-network doctors.**

As you can see from Bert on your right, you might pay **40%** of the costs if you use a doctor *outside* of your network, but only pay **10%** if you stay in-network.

If you are really concerned about which doctors you would go to in the case of a serious accident or illness, then a PPO will give you the greatest flexibility.

Standard PPO Summary
Expensive, but flexible.
You have no PCP to visit.
You can go in- or out-of-network.

PPO example

**out-of-network doctor:
you pay 40%**

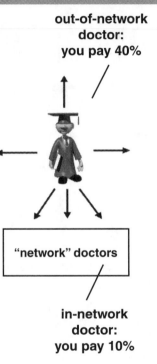

"network" doctors

**in-network doctor:
you pay 10%**

Get friendly

When you move, you not only get new friends and a new grocery store, but you get a new doctor as well. Many people forget this.

When you move or start a new health insurance plan, immediately get to know your new "Dr. Friendly" (PCP / general physician). Start your relationship early.

We know this can be difficult, but consider making an appointment for a general physical with your new doctor.

Call your old doctor and get your health records forwarded. It is better to do it now when you are feeling fine than wait until you are a flu-ridden, sniveling mess in need of medicine.

POS diagram

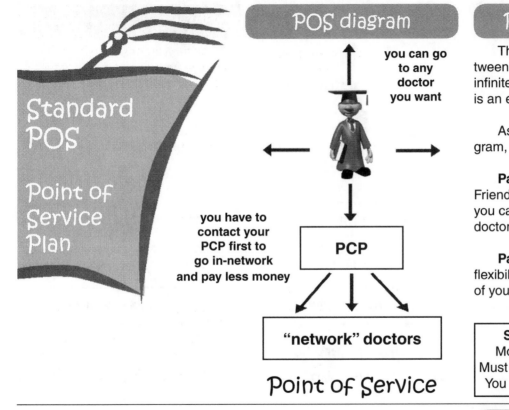

you can go to any doctor you want

you have to contact your PCP first to go in-network and pay less money

PCP

"network" doctors

Point of Service

Standard POS

Point of Service Plan

POS explanation

The variety of plans that fall between an HMO and PPO are nearly infinite. To give you a sample, here is an example of one **POS plan**.

As you can see from the diagram, it's part HMO and part PPO.

Part HMO: You still have Dr. Friendly (PCP) to deal with before you can go to any of the in-network doctors.

Part PPO: You still have the flexibility to go to any doctor outside of your network, for an added cost.

Standard POS Summary
Moderate price and flexibility.
Must visit your PCP for in-network.
You can go in- or out-of-network.

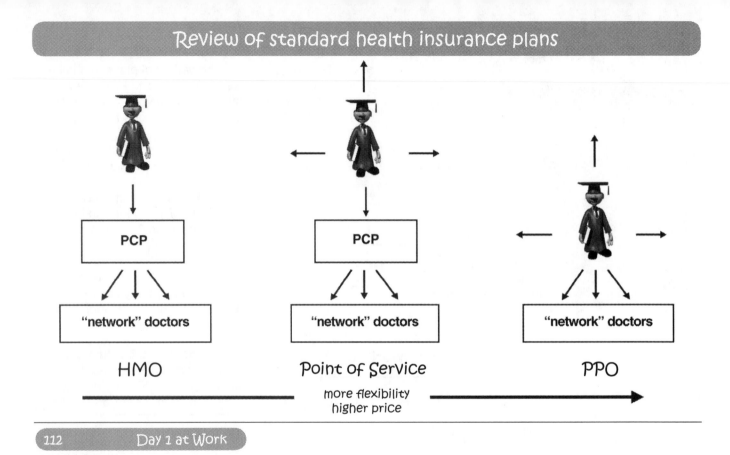

Review of health insurance plans

You've been presented with a number of choices. Which one is best for you?

To start, your employer may offer you a certain plan (usually of the HMO variety) as part of your employment. You may have the option to *upgrade* your plan.

If you are prone to sickness or concerned that you may need the best specialist in the event of an emergency, you may want to consider a more comprehensive plan, like a PPO.

An HMO might be a good choice if you are on a tight budget and aren't as concerned about your coverage.

Remember that you can usually only change your plan once a year. Try to be very selective about your choices now.

If you're at work without your handy Cap & Compass book, you may forget which plan is best. Use this immature mnemonic device to remember that a PPO is usually the *best* plan:

PPO   HMO

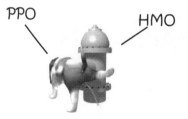

A PPO can "pee-pee" on an HMO.
(As they say, potty humor is always a good memory device.)

Short-term insurance coverage

Your employer may not offer you health insurance until you've been on the job for three months ... or sometimes may not offer it at all.

You may think to yourself, "Nothing is going to happen." Not surprisingly, the mysterious forces behind Murphy's Law seem to culminate during gaps in insurance coverage.

Fortunately, you can get **short-term coverage** for up to six months while you're in between coverages.

Short-term insurance is intended to cover you in the event of an emergency, like a visit to the hospital.

The **premiums**, or monthly payments, *are usually cheaper* than normal health insurance.

It's usually *easier to get short-term coverage.* The provider will usually not ask you as many questions about your health.

Your deductible is *per incident or illness.* Most long-term plans will have a deductible *for the year*, but short-term coverage is *per incident*. Each incident will cost you money out of your pocket.

If you're not offered insurance, you can purchase the same insurance offered by your previous employer for up to 18 months (this is called **COBRA**). If you don't have a previous job, check the phone book under, well, "insurance."

Special
health
insurance
deals

Many employers offer flexible spending accounts, or **flex accounts**, as another perk. Not enough people know what these are for or how to take advantage of them.

A flex account is the equivalent of a big "discount sticker" on your medical bills.

On your first day, your HR rep will ask you how much you'd like to put in your flex account.

Let's assume you say, "$1000." Your employer will gradually take money out of your paycheck until $1000 comes out over the course of the year.

When the money comes out of your paycheck, Uncle Sam never gets the chance to take any of it. You pay no taxes on it. The money goes directly from your salary into this account. (This deal is no longer exclusive for mobsters.)

Say you have a medical expense, like a prescription to fill. You have to pay some portion of the bill. You can use the money in your flex account to pay for this.

Normally you would have paid for it out of your pocket, but now your flex account pays for it and you are the coolest person in the office.

A flex account is like a discount sticker because you are using money that has never been taxed.

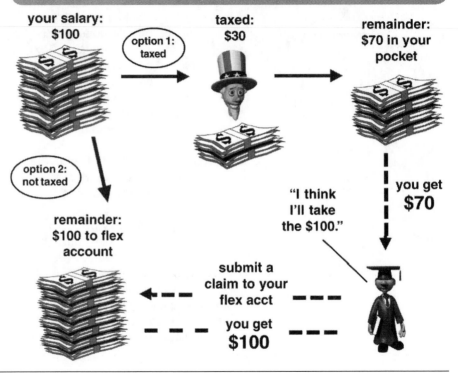

Flex Accts (Cont.)

If flex accounts still don't make any sense, look at the diagram to the right.

A flex account is great, so what's the catch? **If you don't use it, you lose it.** If you don't spend your $1000 by the end of the year, you lose your money.

That said, you should ask your HR representative exactly what medical expenses you can pay for using your flex account.

Then figure out how much money you spend on contact lenses, glasses, or doctor visits over a year. Contribute only the amount you think you'll spend. (*Note:* Some complain that getting paid on claims can be a hassle.)

Two options when paying medical expenses

your salary:
$100

option 1:
taxed

taxed:
$30

remainder:
$70 in your
pocket

option 2:
not taxed

remainder:
$100 to flex
account

"I think
I'll take
the $100."

you get
$70

submit a
claim to your
flex acct

you get
$100

If you're young and healthy, you may opt to spend *less* money (lower premium) by taking a high deductible plan which is often eligible for a health savings account, or HSA. Since this goodie is a great way to save money, we'll tell you how it works.

Set it up. Confirm that you're getting an "HSA-compatible" insurance plan. Then do an online search for banks that offer HSA accounts. This checking account doesn't have to be affiliated with your insurance company.

Fund your HSA account. You can put up to maximum of roughly $3,000 (for an individual) in your checking account. If you contribute more money than you spend in a year, your money stays in your account for the next year (you don't lose it like a flex account).

Spend. Use checks or your debit card to spend money from your account on a large range of allowable medical expenses (including some that your insurance doesn't even cover). The list includes co-pays, prescription and over-the-counter drugs (like allergy medication), dental and vision care, and much more. But in most cases, you can't use your account to pay for monthly premium payments.

The benefits. You indirectly save 10% to 35% on the medical expenses used with your HSA.

Why? In April, when you file your taxes, you'll be able to take a **deduction** (we talk about this *sexy* word in our taxes chapter) for the money you deposit into your HSA. This benefit could save you hundreds of dollars every year.

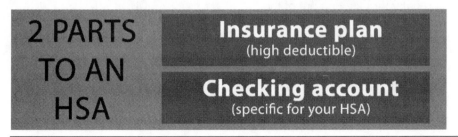

2 PARTS TO AN HSA

Insurance plan
(high deductible)

Checking account
(specific for your HSA)

The 401k: The greatest perk

Here's a simple definition:

A 401k is a company-sponsored plan that allows you to save your money (just like you normally would) **with a bunch of added perks.**

The first question many people ask is, "Why is it called a 401k?"

In our seminars, we always answer the same way: "Why don't you get your lazy butt out of the seat and go look it up? Honestly, people, is learning dead?"

Actually, the real answer is that the government wanted a name that was vague and uninformative, yet still difficult to remember.

Despite the name, a 401k (or a 403b, which is basically the same thing) is a great perk to take advantage of if your employer offers it.

On your first day of work, you'll be asked what percentage of your paycheck you'd like to invest in your 401k.

You are allowed to take up to $15,500 per year and invest this money in different mutual fund choices provided by your employer.

A 401k is not an investment itself, but more like a "special box" for you to keep your mutual funds in (not like some kind of sociopath who likes to *talk* to his "special box," but just a nice, regular box).

This box is special because it allows your money to grow tax-free until you take it out. When money grows tax-free, it grows much more quickly than a taxed investment.

Here's another nice benefit of a 401k:

Good for no self-control

Many of you have no self-control when it comes to your money. Admit it. You save money like the end of the world is Tuesday.

But if money comes out of your paycheck before you even see it, then no harm is done. This is an opportunity for you to save your money without even doing anything.

Drawbacks

Unfortunately, with few exceptions, you can't take your money out of a 401k until you're 59½ (at which time, it *will* get taxed). That's why it's usually called a retirement account.

That being said, you shouldn't just think of a 401k as a retirement account, because that might make you feel sad and old inside.

Think of it more as a birthday present to yourself for turning 60. That way, you will be able to say, "Hi, self, Happy Birthday. Look what I got you. It's enough money to live on for the rest of your life. Wasn't that thoughtful of me?!"

Why worry about saving for retirement now? Surprisingly, worrying now makes a big difference later.

Consider this example. **Bert** puts $2000 into his retirement account (or any investment for that matter) at age 25, then again at 26, and does this every year until age 35. At this point he *stops* investing and leaves his money in the account to earn interest.

invests $2000 for 10 years starting at 25

Bert vs. Chuck

Chuck, on the other hand, doesn't start saving until age 35. To make up for lost time, he adds $2000 every year for **30 years**.

invests $2000 for 30 years starting at 35

Now assume each makes 10% on his money every year. This is a big assumption, but it's possible. Plus it illustrates the following point.

The results are in

Who is going to have more money at age 65: Bert and his 10 years or the Chuckman and his 30?

Take a look at this graph. Bert wins by a landslide. Why? Compound interest. His early investment grows on itself so quickly that Chuck never has a chance to catch up.

If you don't believe this simple graph (thanks for the trust), take a look at the numbers on the next page.

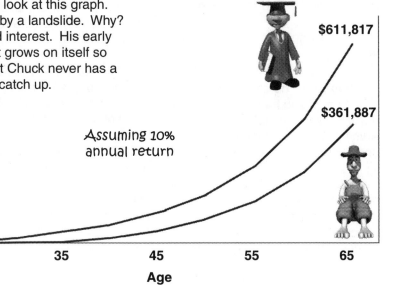

Assuming 10% annual return

$611,817

$361,887

Age: 25 35 45 55 65

Bert vs. Chuck: Behind the scenes

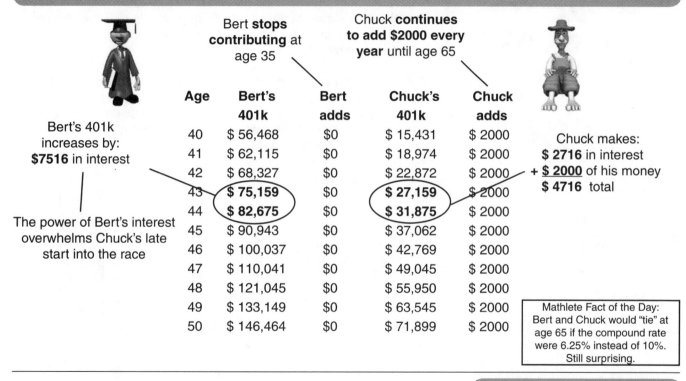

Bert stops contributing at age 35

Chuck continues to add $2000 every year until age 65

Bert's 401k increases by: **$7516** in interest

The power of Bert's interest overwhelms Chuck's late start into the race

Age	Bert's 401k	Bert adds	Chuck's 401k	Chuck adds
40	$ 56,468	$0	$ 15,431	$ 2000
41	$ 62,115	$0	$ 18,974	$ 2000
42	$ 68,327	$0	$ 22,872	$ 2000
43	**$ 75,159**	$0	**$ 27,159**	$ 2000
44	**$ 82,675**	$0	**$ 31,875**	$ 2000
45	$ 90,943	$0	$ 37,062	$ 2000
46	$ 100,037	$0	$ 42,769	$ 2000
47	$ 110,041	$0	$ 49,045	$ 2000
48	$ 121,045	$0	$ 55,950	$ 2000
49	$ 133,149	$0	$ 63,545	$ 2000
50	$ 146,464	$0	$ 71,899	$ 2000

Chuck makes:
$ 2716 in interest
+ **$ 2000** of his money
$ 4716 total

Mathlete Fact of the Day:
Bert and Chuck would "tie" at age 65 if the compound rate were 6.25% instead of 10%. Still surprising.

Matched
401k

To make 401k's even better, sometimes your company will offer a perk called a **matched 401k**.

This means that your company will "match" the amount of money you put into your 401k every year. If you add $100, they'll add $100 with no strings attached (that's a 100% return). The company is essentially giving you a raise without any work on your part (the *best* kind of raise).

There will often be a limit imposed on your match. For example, your company may only match up to 3% of your salary. But who cares? *This is free money.*

Look at the graph below. When you compare this investment to other "non-risk" investments (or to *any* other investments for that matter), it has a great return.

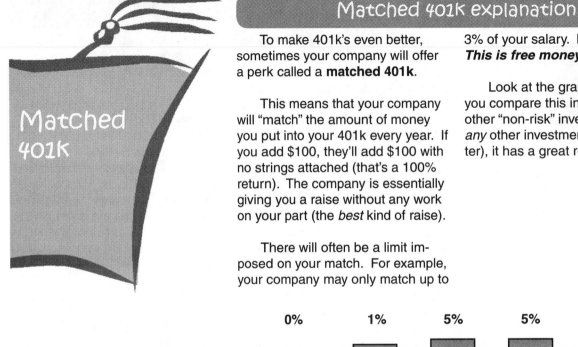

| 0% | 1% | 5% | 5% | 100% |
| checking | savings | money market | CD | 401k match |

That tax form: W-4

When you first start working, your employer will ask you to fill out this confusing form, the W-4. It looks intimidating because it deals with taxes. The word "taxes" scares people. But after you get through this section, you'll see that there's no reason to fear.

The W-4 form lets you decide *when* you want to pay your taxes to Uncle Sam.

He's either going to take *too much* out of each paycheck and then pay you back at the end of the year, or he'll take *too little* out of each paycheck and you'll owe him some in April.

Either way, Uncle Sam will get what's coming to him. That's why we have Tax Day, April 15th. It's Uncle Sam's chance to settle the score.

Many people always put zero on the form because they like to get back a refund at the end of the year.

Let's discuss why this is the *worst* idea in the world and actually causes government officials to openly mock and scoff your W-4 form.

Form W-4

Purpose. Complete Form W-4 so that your employer can withhold the correct federal income tax from your pay. Because your tax situation may change, you may want to refigure your withholding each year.

Exemption from withholding. If you are exempt, complete only lines 1, 2, 3, 4, and 7 and sign the form to validate it. Your exemption for 2006 expires February 16, 2007. See Pub. 505, Tax

Decoding the W-4 form (the top half)

Personal Allowances Worksheet (Keep for your records.)

A Enter "1" for **yourself** if no one else can claim you as a dependent . . . .   **A** _____

B Enter "1" if:
- You are single and have only one job; or
- You are married, have only one job, and your spouse does not work; or
- Your wages from a second job or your spouse's wages (or the total of both) are $1,000 or less.

  B _____

To start off, there are two parts to the form. The top half is called the **Personal Allowances Worksheet** because that's what it is: a worksheet.

This part will give you some *suggestions* about how you should fill out the bottom half of the form, but your employer will not get the worksheet. It doesn't count.

At the same time, you shouldn't write something like, "My boss is a big weiner" or "Never eat yellow snow."

For most people coming out of school, the only two lines that really matter to you are lines A and B.

For **Line A**, Uncle Sam is asking if *you* are the one paying the bills (rent and food). If you're paying your bills, then you put down a "1."

If by some chance your parents are still paying your bills, then NICE WORK. Please write to us at:

Feedback@CapandCompass.com

and explain your method. You'll

need to put down a "0." You may want to ask your folks if they're claiming you as a **dependent**, but most likely, you'll be putting a "1" on Line A.

Line B is actually pretty straight forward. You're probably single with one job, so put down a "1."

This worksheet suggests for most of you to put down a total of two **allowances**. Remember, this worksheet is just a *suggestion*. On the *bottom half*, you can put down whatever you want (to a point).

Why refunds are a bad idea (W-4)

The problem with a refund is that in order to get any money back at the end of the year, you'll had to have paid too much in taxes over the course of the year. The refund was your money from the start. It's like getting your old sweater as a birthday gift. Thanks, Mom!

To make matters worse, Uncle Sam **earns interest** on *your money* while he holds it and *never passes this interest onto you.*

Only a "zero" would put a zero on a W-4.

If you've put down a zero in the past, we still affirm you as a person, but you should change your habits.

In most cases, **you should put down at least one or two on your W-4**. Otherwise, you're passing up an opportunity to earn interest on your own money.

Unfortunately, Uncle Sam doesn't allow you to claim 45 allowances and earn interest on all of *his* money (he's funny that way). If you put down too many allowances, it will raise a red IRS flag. Stick with one or two.

You'll pay too much in taxes during the year, but get it back in April.

The diagram on the right recaps this explanation with cute little pictures (for those "visual learners").

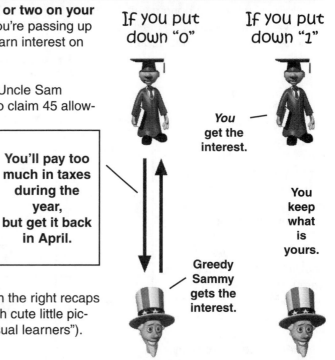

If you put down "0"

If you put down "1"

You get the interest.

You keep what is yours.

Greedy Sammy gets the interest.

Now we get to the bottom half of the W-4 where you get to make a choice. Oh joy! For most recent grads:

If you put down "2" you'll *underpay* your taxes each pay period. You'll pay a small amount of each paycheck to Uncle Sam. Since you paid too little, you'll make up the difference by paying Uncle Sam at the end of the year.

If you put down "1" you'll likely pay an *accurate* amount of taxes from each paycheck. You'll pay a little more in taxes than if you put down two. Since you were accurate, there likely won't be much of a payment at the end of the year.

If you put down "0" you'll likely pay *too much* in taxes each pay period. You'll pay a *larger* amount in taxes to Uncle Sam from each paycheck. Since you paid *too much*, you'll get a refund at the end of the year.

What should you do?

The general public seems to cheer the idea of getting money back at the end of the year. This happens when you put down zero.

But let's be honest, the general public made Carmen Electra a household name. Does anyone know why? Really, we'd like to know.

# of allowances	you pay from your paycheck	you pay at tax time
2	💵	💵
1	💵	—
0	💵	**refund**

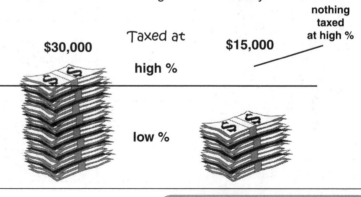

Part-year method on a W-4

Part-year method explanation

Here's another nice little tip about your W-4. Most of you will probably be starting your first job over the summer, which is midyear.

If your salary is $30,000, your income for this calendar year will only be $15,000 (you're working for half of the year).

Uncle Sam doesn't know this unless you tell him. He'll see $30,000 and tax you in a higher tax bracket. You'll get that money back at the end of the year, but he'll keep the interest he earned on your money. Bad, Uncle Sam. Bad.

Simply tell your HR representative that you'd like the "part-year method" on your W-4. Then you'll get taxed correctly.

$30,000   Taxed at   **$15,000**   nothing taxed at high %

high %

low %

HR rep? Don't you love this page?
See IRS Publication 15a, Chapter 9

Work etiquette

Overview

In our "Avoid Looking Stupid at Dinner" chapter, we mentioned that *personal* skills often have a larger impact on your job success than your technical skills.

Since we at Cap & Compass want all of our readers to become successful superstars, we occasionally do some informal polling of companies who hire a lot of new college graduates. Where could your new hires improve?

These next few columns provide some inside scoop. Between these tips and your charming personality, you'll be CEO of the company in no time at all.

Personal touch

Bert received a brief email from his boss: "That's nice."

That's *nice*? Was that a compliment or is she just patronizing me? Yes, she might be more senior than me, but I'm really smart. "That's nice." Who does she think she is?!

How can something as harmless as "that's nice" in an email send someone into a tizzy? We're not even sure what a tizzy is.

 Email, chat, and texting just doesn't do a good job capturing the nuances of a conversation, like voice inflection and body language.

Personal (Cont.)

Instead of using those uber-professional emoticons to bridge the gap, focus on more in-person or verbal communications on the job.

If someone asks for a "live" meeting, give them a live meeting. A voicemail should be returned with a voicemail or live meeting, but never with email or text.

Over the past few years, the biggest complaint that we've heard from companies about college new hires is their **over reliance of technology in communication**.

Show your new colleagues your amazing personality and communication skills. Walk over to their desk and show them your pearly whites instead of sending them an email.

Responding

After the personal touch, the second biggest complaint from employers is the responsiveness from college new hires.

Be timely. You may look desperate if you call the girl 24 hours after getting her number, but you look *professional* when you reply to a request quickly at work. Never let 24 hours go by without at least acknowledging a request or question.

No response. If you're unable to do something or be somewhere, it's ok to respond with a no. You lose points when you never respond to a request or question in the workplace.

Blogs

Since Bert knows that he's the center of the universe, he posts weekly messages on his blog about his favorite TV show and cereal.

After the huge "that's nice" email drama, he wrote some "not-so-nice" comments about her on his blog. Since no one at work ever reads it, he didn't think it would be a problem, until someone did.

After a meeting with his human resources representative, Bert learned about his company's strict public blogging policies. "It's a free country, but your employer is free to fire you, too," he later wrote.

If your blog mentions work, get permission. Or, just be smart and complain to your roommate instead.

Your friend might enjoy your *crazy* Santa hat smily face in emails, but all email rules change once you're on the job.

Get to the point. Keep your emails brief, avoid long sentences and paragraphs, and try to answer questions before they are asked.

Fonts. As the philospher Plato once said, "An email font is the window to your soul, so choose wisely." If the decision is yours, use Times New Roman to say, "I conform." Verdana tells people that you're trying to be different in that non-Harley Davidson kind of way. Kristin ITC suggests that you'd rather be eating ice cream.

Emphasis. Don't overuse the high priority option and nothing deserves four explanation points!!!! Plus, too many explanation points can trigger email spam filters.

Proofread. As thoughts flow out of your head, they inevitably stumble a few times out of your fingers. Always reread your emails before they are sent. Spellcheck will not pick up errors like "Did you like my massage?"

Capitalization. Everyone loves free expression, but for business emails, keep your inner artist away from the caps lock. capitalize the beginning of your sentences and DON'T SCREAM WITH ALL CAPS.

Personal use. When you quickly minimize your browser every time your boss visits your desk, it's obvious that you're on Gmail or Facebook. Do the personal stuff on your watch.

Attachments. Keep them small. Big ones are annoying.

Reply all. Everyone in your office does not need to know your every thought, so use the "reply all" sparingly. And everyone hates the guy who uses "reply all" to get removed from a group email.

Play it safe. An offensive or obscene email never goes away. A virus downloaded from your personal email account can affect everyone in the office. Be thoughtful with your email use at work.

The Least You Need to Know About Taxes

"After FICA, Social Security, Federal and state taxes,
your allowance comes to 18 cents."

The Least You Need to Know About Taxes

For most people, taxes top the list of "Things I Didn't Know Anything About When I Graduated." It also tops other lists, like "Reasons to Shove a Spike in My Head."

While in college, most people gave their tax forms to their parents' accountant, paid $50, and everything was magically completed.

Your conversation with a tax accountant is usually similar to your conversation with a car mechanic:

"Your left, forward axel and suspension gaskets need fixing. That's going to cost you."

"Right. That's *exactly* what I *thought* it was."

Many people have no idea what is happening, so they are happy to shell out $50 or $100 each year to make the problem go away.

Alternatively, if you learn the very *least* that you need to know about taxes, you'll become a little bit smarter about the process.

You may still elect to have someone else do the job at the end of the year, but at least you'll have a better idea of what's happening to your money.

If all goes well, you'll have enough courage to file taxes yourself. At the very least, you may save an extra receipt here or there that saves you enough money for a movie on a Friday night.

Learning the very *least* you need to know means that you won't be learning everything. This book would be a lot thicker (and use far bigger words) if taxes were explained in full.

We're not going to go into every miserable detail, because, well, the details are miserable. If you wanted miserable, you could have turned on any old Keanu Reeves movie. Plus, many tax laws are very specific to individual cases.

For example, did you know that you can save money in taxes if you are over 65 and blind? More importantly, a 65-year-old blind man can save money in taxes by using a *guide dog* instead of a walking stick. (We always want to take care of our 65-year-old blind readers out there. Word.)

With that said, if you have any specific or more complicated tax questions, you should refer to a tax accountant or a giant tax book. Remember to keep all large spikes out of reach (or wear a strong helmet). You'll thank us later.

But if you'd like to get a great foundation on taxes that won't put you to sleep, this chapter will set you on the right path.

If any part of this chapter starts to bore you, please refer to page 174.

Uncle Sam has already made a few appearances in this book, but we haven't given him a proper introduction. For those of you who don't know, this is Uncle Sam (or Sammy, to close personal friends):

Originally, he was depicted extending his pinky, as in "I want YOU to make a pinky swear that you'll be the bestest friend I ever had," but the government decided to go with something more mature, like the "pull my finger" gesture.

W-4 form

When you start your first job as a professional wrestler or consultant or whatever, your employer is going to ask you to fill out a W-4.

We just discussed this form (in more detail) in the previous chapter. This is the form with the "0," "1," and "2," that always confuses people because no one ever really knows what to do. You are expected just to magically *know*.

"Val, my wonderful human resources representative, what number should I put down here?"

"Well, that's up to you."

"Umm, ok."

Now you'll have it magically *written down and explained*. The W-4 form lets you decide *when* you want to pay your taxes to Uncle Sam. He's either going to take *too much* out of each paycheck and then pay you back at the end of the year, or he'll take out *too little,* and you'll owe Uncle Sam a little bit in April. That's why everyone has to file taxes by April 15th: to settle the score with Uncle Sam.

To cut to the chase, if you're just coming out of school and you're single, you'll most likely want to put down "1" on the form. With "1" on the form, you'll likely come out pretty even at the end of the year. You won't owe Uncle Sam much, and he won't owe you much either.

When you first start working, you'll likely be getting a paycheck, unless you take a job in education (or a job starting a company about "life after school").

For many people, their first payday was a shocker. They weren't expecting to give away 30% of their money to things like Social Security.

Don't get us wrong. Everyone is certainly pro-elderly, especially the Democratic and Republican parties during election years. But once you get your first paycheck, you want to corner every old person you see and start yelling at them, "Give me my money back!" (We love you, Grandma.)

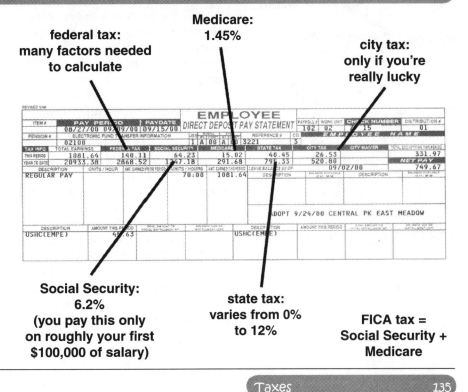

federal tax:
many factors needed to calculate

Medicare:
1.45%

city tax:
only if you're really lucky

Social Security:
6.2%
(you pay this only on roughly your first $100,000 of salary)

state tax:
varies from 0% to 12%

FICA tax =
Social Security + Medicare

Who has to file taxes?

Now that you know what comes out of your paycheck, you should also know that getting a paycheck *pretty much* means you have to file taxes.

In addition to paying federal (or national) taxes, the state, and sometimes even the city, likes to get its cut, too. No one wants to miss the party. The forms used for **state taxes** vary from state to state, but most will look similar to the federal ones we'll talk about later.

What happens if you don't file? Sooner or later, you'll get caught. Like the saying goes, "Don't mess with taxes." Or is it Wyoming? No, we're pretty sure it's taxes. If you get a paycheck, you probably need to file taxes, so don't mess around.

The problem with not filing (besides the illegality) is that you're never off the hook for the money you owe. Once you file, the statute of limitations for the IRS to audit you is generally three years.

Additionally, if you ever want to buy a home, you'll likely need to get a mortgage. Your bank will need to look at your past tax records to determine how much money you've been earning. When you show up at the bank with an empty box, they'll probably notice that something's wrong. Then you'll have to answer to the IRS (when the bank turns you in), possibly pay fines, go to prison, blah, blah, blah.

The two piles of money

When you're hired, your employer is going to give you a starting salary. Let's assume that's $30,000 a year.

At the end of the year when you settle the score with Uncle Sam, the government won't tax you on $30,000. Instead, they may only tax you on $22,000. Why is that?

This is the most important idea in this tax chapter:

The money you make is *different* from the money they tax.

Two important piles of money exist: one pile called **Money You Make** and the other called **Money They Tax**.

The whole exercise of filing taxes involves making your "Money They Tax" pile as small as (legally) possible.

That's why your parents spend afternoons in April looking for receipts in the garbage. They're trying to find ways to make their income look really small to Uncle Sam so that they can save money in taxes.

Money You Make
(gross income)

Money They Tax
(taxable income)

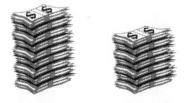

Why two piles?

Why is there a difference between your salary and the Money They Tax? Why don't they just give you a salary, tax it, and call it a day?

For two reasons:

Bribery

Everyone knows the best way to influence a ref in a big game. Everyone knows how to get a good table in a restaurant. Some people call it "bribery," but Uncle Sam calls it a "tax break." Yes, the US government plays the same games we do.

Uncle Sam bribes you to be a good citizen. He sets up random standards for "good citizenship," like buying a home, going to school, or supporting a charity. Do the right things, and he'll slip you some extra dough (fair enough).

Compassion

Believe it or not, Uncle Sam wants to help you. He'll give you a tax break if you have some giant financial burden, some huge medical expense, or some kids.

The government decided, "Hey, if we give people tax breaks, maybe they won't hate us so much for making them pay in the first place."

We couldn't agree more.

Those sexy words

As I'm sure you can imagine, a lot of time and research went into putting this book together. Everyone at Cap & Compass spent hours reading tax books and talking to accountants, just so that we could best explain the tax system to you.

In our conversations with accountants, we asked them, "What aspect of filing taxes really *turns you on*?"

Time and time again, accountants told us that they get all hot and bothered when they hear the words "dependents," "deductions," and "retirement accounts." They're smoking!

These are the sexy words:

- **Dependents**
- **Deductions**
- **Retirement accounts**

They might not sound attractive to you now, but they'll be on fire when you're filing taxes. They are the sexy words of accounting that make your income look smaller to Uncle Sam.

Remember how we mentioned that the goal of filing taxes is to turn the first pile into a really small second pile?

These are the words that are going to get you there. They're going to save you money.

Sexy word:

Dependents

The first word, **dependent**, refers to someone who *depends* on you for money. Put more simply:

A dependent is a mouth to feed.

Usually this means that we're talking about a kid. A dependent could also mean someone else who lives in your home (your grandpa).

So what is a kid (or mouth) worth to Uncle Sam? You may think to yourself, "I'm certainly more charming than my brother, and I spent at least $10 on that goober for Christmas. I'm worth $79,000."

Unfortunately, Uncle Sam doesn't know who the goobers are, so he assigns one number to all of you. For the 2008 tax year, that number is: **$3500**.

You might be thinking to yourself, "Wait, I don't have any kids. How does this affect me?"

Even if you don't have any kids, Uncle Sam still gives you credit for *one* dependent. He figures that your income pays for one mouth: *your own*. (Actually, a dependent credit for yourself is called an even *sexier* word: **exemption**.) Is it getting hot in here, or is it just us?!

For this reason, if you don't depend on your parents for food and shelter, you get $3500 off your pile. *How 'bout that Uncle Sam!*

Sexy word:

Deductions

Deductions explanation

 The word **deduction** covers *all the other tax breaks* (besides a mouth to feed) that Uncle Sam gives away.

Remember how we said that Uncle Sam *helps us* in tough times and *bribes us* to be good citizens?

Instead of sitting down with each of us and listening to our stories like a shopping mall Santa, he gives us the benefit of the doubt. He assumes that we've run into *some* tough times and done *some* good things over the course of the year.

In the 2008 tax year, he gives everyone an unconditional tax break of **$5450** for single folks. *Man is this guy great!*

You don't have to do anything, and you get an additional $5450 off of the "Money You Make" pile on top of the $3500 you took earlier. If we keep up this pace, Uncle Sam is going to be paying *you* taxes by the end of this book. This is called the

standard deduction.

Why $5450? Who knows. It's the government.

Once you get old and mature, you'll start to collect more good deeds in the eyes of Uncle Sam. At that point, you'll be able **itemize** (or list) your tough times and good deeds.

If the *total of your list* is greater than $5450, then you can subtract *this* amount from your pile instead of the standard deduction.

What does Uncle Sam deem worthy to put on your list? The list is so random and huge that you'd need to buy a 300-page book to see all of the possibilities. Go into any bookstore and you'll have ten choices.

Some of the biggest "items" that you can put on your list to get above the $5450 threshold are:

- **interest paid on a mortgage**
- **gifts to charity**
- **state taxes**
- **real estate taxes**

If you don't own your own home or make a six-figure salary, it probably won't make sense to itemize, because your list will be too small.

Most people coming out of school just take the standard deduction.

Once you start paying interest on a mortgage or have a huge medical expense, you may want to consult with an accountant in order to make sure that you make your list as long as possible.

Otherwise, if you're like most people coming out of school, just take your $5450 and run. You're a good person. You deserve it.

Let's review. You have two piles, the Money You Make and the Money They Tax. Your mission, should you choose to accept it, is to make the second pile as small as possible using your "sexy words."

So far, you've dropped the pile $3500 for one dependent (exemption) and an additional $5450 for your standard deduction. Plus, you have one more sexy word to go.

Money You Make

Money They Tax

dependents
deductions

Sexy word:

Retirement accounts

It's not often that you hear people singing the praises of Uncle Sam's tax system, but get ready: we're warming up our vocal chords.

One great thing about Uncle Sam's system is that he built an express lane for retirement savings.

He allows us to earmark a certain amount of our money for retirement in a "special box" called a **401k**, a **403b**, or an **IRA** (Individual Retirement Account).

These aren't investments themselves. They're more like special boxes where you can put your investments. Within these boxes,

your investments get all sorts of special powers. Most importantly:

Your money grows tax-free until you're old and gray.

What's so great about that? When your money grows tax-free, your account grows much more quickly than any normal account. You are earning more interest on your interest (**compound interest**).

Think of your retirement account as the *"Lebron James" of investments*. It's faster and stronger than any other type of investment, because you're not taxed on it every year.

If you had to pick one teammate to help you win the McKean YMCA

Five on Five Thursday Night Hoops Tourney, whom would you pick?

Would you go with Tony Parker and his desperate housewife? No.

How about Dwayne Wade and his fave five? He might save you money on your cellphone plan, but that won't help you in the big game.

Or would you go with King James who could hit 90 foot threes while posing for the cover of McKean Weekly? The choice is clear.

Someone in our seminars raised his hand in one of our seminars and said, "But what does Lebron know about 401(k)'s?"

True. Work with us.

Most retirement accounts work the same way. You choose your investment (usually a mutual fund) and put it in your "special box."

At the end of the year, you tell Uncle Sam about your box, and he'll return the money that he "wrongfully" taxed you.

For example, let's look at $2000 of your salary. Suppose that you only got $1400 of that amount in your paycheck due to taxes.

You set up your special box called an IRA and invest $2000 in your choice of mutual funds.

Since your $2000 in salary earnings went into a retirement account (which is not taxed now), Uncle Sam will give you back the $600 that he originally took from your paycheck. What a guy!

Normal investments get taxed every year. Retirement accounts just sit nice and pretty in their special boxes and keep growing and growing with compound interest.

When you withdraw your money, you'll finally get taxed on it. (Sooner or later he'll get his money.) But at this point, your money has already outgrown a comparable investment in a regular, boring taxed account.

Special rules for retirement accounts

These are called "retirement accounts" because normally:

You can't get to your money until you're 59 1/2.

You'll be able to use the money for early bird specials and a new TV to watch Matlock. You'll be charged a 10% penalty if you take it out early.

But never fear! Like all good rules, it has exceptions that might be relevant to you. If you are:

paying for college or buying your first home

you can take money out of an IRA early without paying penalties, but you'll get taxed. (Sooner or later, it was going to happen.)

You can only contribute up to $5000 per year into an IRA (2008 tax year).

But the more money you make, the less Uncle Sam allows you to contribute to an IRA. Why? Uncle Sam was in a bad mood on the day he wrote that tax law.

Company-sponsored plans, like **401k's**, allow you to contribute more of your salary each year (up to $15,500 in 2008).

These are just a few of the rules attached to retirement accounts. Once again, nothing is simple when it comes to taxes. But these things are the *least* you need to know.

Getting one

If you want to get an IRA, you simply go on-line (or visit a bank).

Step 1: Pick virtually any on-line broker or mutual fund. A list of choices can be found on pages 64 and 65.

Step 2: Click on "Open an IRA account." It's getting tricky.

Step 3: Select a mutual fund (or stocks) to invest in. These are now in your "special box."

Step 4: Yell loudly, "Hey Uncle Sam! Na-na-na-na-na-na, you can't touch me!"

Step 5: Print out your application form, sign it, and send that puppy in. It's that simple.

Special deductions: ideal for college grads

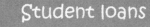

There are two deductions ideal for college graduates. The first is the **student loan interest deduction.**

If you have any student loans, you can get a tax break at the end of the year from Uncle Sam.

- You can get up to $2500 a year in tax deductions (to make your "Money They Tax" pile smaller).

- If you're single, this benefit starts to disappear once you make $50,000 and disappears completely at $65,000.

See IRS Publication 970 for more information.

If you move more than 50 miles from your former home (like many new graduates), you can get a tax break from Uncle Sam for the moving expenses your employer doesn't pick up.

The **moving deduction** gets more complicated in the rules category: You need to be employed for 39 out of the next 52 weeks, you can count the cost of lodging and a moving van, but not meals, blah, blah, blah. (See tax form 3903.)

The great thing about these two deductions is that *you don't have to itemize to use them.* **You can add them to your standard deduction.**

Tax brackets

Once you've reduced your "Money They Tax" pile to as little as possible, you'll need to identify the **tax bracket** you fall into.

Tax brackets are Uncle Sam's way of taking his cut. He believes that the more money you make, the more he can tax. You can see the full brackets on the next page for single and married folks.

Fortunately, Uncle Sam doesn't tax *all* of your money at a particular rate. Rather, he only taxes *slivers* of money at particular "bracketed" rates. Huh?

Take a look at the example below. Try to imagine that the "Money They Tax" pile is $22,000 for you.

"Money They Tax" pile
$22,000

Of your $22,000...

15%

only **$13,975**
is taxed at **15%**

$8,025

10%

the first **$8,025**
is taxed at **10%**

Tax brackets

Single

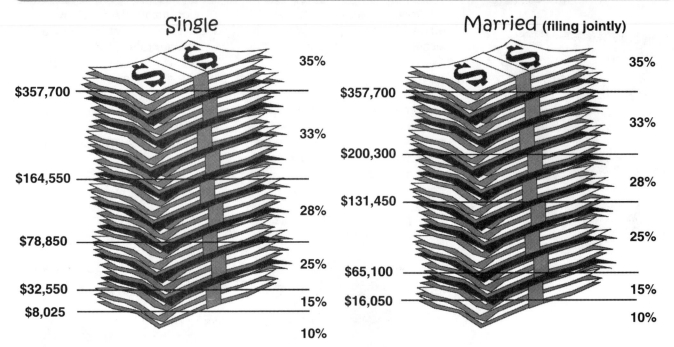

$357,700 ——— 35%

$164,550 ——— 33%

$78,850 ——— 28%

$32,550 ——— 25%

$8,025 ——— 15%

10%

Married (filing jointly)

$357,700 ——— 35%

$200,300 ——— 33%

$131,450 ——— 28%

$65,100 ——— 25%

$16,050 ——— 15%

10%

The above rates are used when filing your taxes in April of 2009 (the 2008 tax year). The brackets may vary slightly each year.

Holding periods for stocks

When you buy or own a stock, you are only taxed *once you sell it* (with a few exceptions, of course).

If you bought a stock for $1000 and then sold it for $2000, Uncle Sam pretends like you earned (or **realized**) an extra $1000 of salary. So instead of paying taxes based on your $22,000 "Money They Tax" pile, you pay taxes on $23,000. Simple enough.

But, if you owned that stock for *more than a year* before you sold it, Uncle Sam cuts you a break.

Once again, Uncle Sam rewards you for being a good citizen (you're adding to market stability). We said he had some arbitrary standards. He taxes you at only 5% instead of your regular 15% rate*.

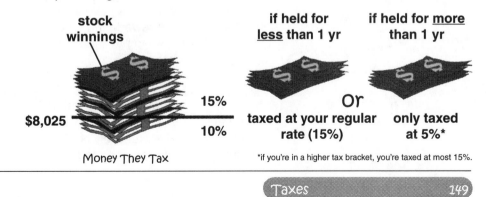

stock winnings

$8,025

15%

10%

Money They Tax

if held for <u>less</u> than 1 yr

if held for <u>more</u> than 1 yr

Or

taxed at your regular rate (15%)

only taxed at 5%*

*if you're in a higher tax bracket, you're taxed at most 15%.

Filing your taxes

Your options

Pay a tax accountant

If you have a fairly uncomplicated tax life, you'll likely pay anywhere between $50 and $100. You can go to a big chain like H&R Block or any of a gazillion tax accountants. Look in the phone book under, um, "tax accountants."

Computer program

TurboTax and TaxCut are the two most popular programs on the market. Both are easy to use (it's like being interviewed) and under $50. You'll need to pay for a new version each year.

Do them yourself

Filing yourself is the only free method. If you don't have a very complicated tax life, you'll be surprised at how simple this is.

Getting forms

Should you decide to accept the challenge of filing yourself, you'll be able to get the forms from a variety of places starting in January of each year:

- **Libraries**
- **Post offices**
- **1-800-TAX-FORM**

We also recommend the IRS website at: **www.IRS.gov.**

This is a surprisingly user-friendly site that provides easy access to all forms.

So which forms do you need?

You'll need to send in either a 1040, 1040A, or 1040EZ tax form postmarked by April 15th.

One of them is actually called the 1040EZ. This is Uncle Sam's lame attempt to try to fit in with the kids these days. He wanted to be "hip" and "bad," so he named it the EZ form. It's one page and is the easiest of the three forms to fill out.

The 1040A is a little more complicated (two pages), and the 1040 can be an animal.

Unfortunately, not everyone is allowed to fill out the "EZ" one.

Which forms are needed?

Which form?

1040EZ

The 1040EZ is the easiest form to fill out, but it offers fewer opportunities for you to reduce your taxes.

In order to be allowed to fill out the 1040EZ, Uncle Sam created a laundry list of requirements. The highlights include:

- **Your "Money They Tax" pile is less than $100,000**
- **No kids** (dependents)
- **No investment earnings** (beyond $1500 in interest)
- **Not adding to an IRA**
- **Not itemizing** (no list)
- **No student loan interest deduction**
- **No moving deduction**

When you get your form, the instructions will have the full list.

Who is a good example of someone who would file a 1040EZ?

A recent graduate.

Most new graduates aren't making a whole lot of money (except on their laser jet printers), don't have any kids (besides baby goats), and don't have any investments (Do Pokemon cards count?).

If this is the case, you should strongly consider filing taxes yourself. You'd be surprised at how easy this is. (We'll show you soon.)

Which form?

1040A

Who can file it

The bouncers at Club "1040A" are a little more strict about letting people in the doors. However, as long as you're not wearing jeans and you meet this abbreviated list of requirements, you'll get past the velvet rope.

- **Your "Money They Tax" pile is less than $100,000**
- **No sale of stock**
- **No itemizing** (no list)
- **No running with scissors**

Once again, the full list of requirements can be found in the instructions for the 1040A form.

If you didn't pass the cool test for the 1040EZ or 1040A, you'll have to tackle the bad boy called the 1040.

Example

Who is a good example of someone who would file a 1040A?

Snow White. She'd prefer to fill out the 1040EZ, but she has seven dwarfs running around as dependents. If you have dependents (or extra mouths to feed), you can't file the 1040EZ.

Is her "Money They Tax" pile less than $100,000? Probably. She hangs out in the woods picking apples all day, for goodness' sake.

She probably isn't selling any stock, since it's hard to access E*Trade in the middle of an enchanted forest.

She is classic 1040A.

Which form?

1040

Who can file it

Anyone can file the 1040. But most people prefer the other two forms because they're easier.

If you fall into any of the following categories for the tax year, you *have* to file the 1040:

- **Your "Money They Tax" pile is greater than $100,000**
- **You're itemizing** (your list)
- **You're claiming the moving deduction**
- **You've sold stocks**

The 1040 is a little more complicated than the other two forms. But the upside is that you'll have more opportunities to save money in taxes.

Example

Who is a good example of someone who would file a 1040?

Count Dracula, the legendary vampire and ladies' man.

Was his "Money They Tax" pile more than $100,000? He's a count and lives in a huge castle, so sure, he's probably making plenty of money, um, "counting."

Did Dracula need to itemize? He has a lot of business expenses: capes, coffins, horse-drawn carriages, henchmen to drive horse-drawn carriages, and maybe a servant to break all the mirrors in the castle.

For these reasons, Count Dracula is your classic 1040 filer.

W-2 form

Depending how complicated your tax life might be, you'll either need a little or lot of paperwork come tax time. No matter what, you'll need to have a copy of your **financial report card** from your employer, called a **W-2**.

This form describes what you made for the year and how much you paid in taxes. Your employer is required to send you one of these at the end of the year.

Don't lose your W-2. If you lose this important form, you'll have to call your employer's accounting division and request another form. Your accounting division will hate you.

If you call and ask them to send you a new W-2, they'll treat you like you're asking for a major organ: "Hi, I seem to have misplaced my pancreas. Could I borrow yours? I'll be gentle."

Don't lose your W-2.

16 State	Employer's state I.D. no.	17 State

Form W-2 Wage and Tax Statement **20**

Copy 1 For State, City, or Local Tax Depar

1040EZ

If you're in the 1040EZ category, you have an easy road ahead of you. You won't need very much paperwork.

- **W-2 form**
- **Tax forms sent by your bank** (interest from savings, etc.)

This applies whether you're doing your own taxes or handing them over to someone else (lazy bum).

Actually, if someone else is doing them, you'll also want to bring your **checkbook**. Write on the comments line of your check, "I was too lazy to fill out the 1040EZ myself. Here's my money."

1040A

Life is slowly getting more difficult. Make sure you have:

- **W-2 form**
- **Tax forms sent by your bank**
- **Student loan receipts**
- **IRA contributions**

Remember: If the IRS ever audits you (checks your math), you'll need your receipts, or they'll kick you in the kneecaps.

You'll need to keep your receipts for a minimum of *three years*. After three years, you're generally off the hook for any errors you may have committed.

1040

If you're a 1040 filer, you're going to need a lot of receipts. You'll need to keep:

- **W-2 form**
- **Tax forms sent by your bank**
- **Student loan receipts**
- **IRA contributions**
- **Donation receipts**
- **Moving receipts**
- **Mortgage interest receipts**
- **Stock sale receipts**
- **Dirty underwear**

Keep anything and everything. If you're organized with your receipts, you'll have a beautiful and enjoyable filing experience.

Remember when you used to watch the older kids play the game Go Fish and you couldn't quite get the rules?

Filing your taxes is a little like playing Go Fish, but now you're old enough to realize that the game isn't really that complicated (or not).

For example, on the 1040EZ, line 1 states, "Total wages, salaries, and tips. This should be shown in box 1 of your W-2 form." You simply get your W-2 and look in box 1.

Besides playing Go Fish on a couple of lines, you'll have to do a little addition and subtraction. For-tunately, Uncle Sam lets you use a calculator.

Since you have a basic un-derstanding of taxes now, you'll be surprised at how simple it is to file a 1040EZ. The 1040A isn't much more difficult. (You'll just have a front and back page now.)

Don't take our word for it. Get the forms and look at them yourself. On the 1040EZ, when it instructs you to take $8950 off your salary, you'll know that this number repre-sents $3500 for your own mouth to feed and $5450 for your standard deduction.

If you need to file the 1040, we recommend that you at least buy a giant tax book or computer software.

Pros and cons of filing yourself

Pros

If you're filing the 1040EZ or 1040A, you should read the instructions and try filing yourself. You'll get these great benefits:

- **Save $50 to $100**
- **Be tax-savvy for next year**
- **Have a great conversation topic for a first date**

If you're still not convinced that you should file on your own, pay someone to do your taxes for you. But you should do them yourself, too. If you get the same answer as the pro, you should feel more comfortable doing them yourself next year.

If you can easily save yourself some money, why not do so?

Cons

There are the few drawbacks:

You might miss a tax trick.

If you're a 1040EZ filer, there aren't too many "tax tricks" available to you. If you're filing a 1040, this point might be valid, and you might want to consider a tax accountant.

You might make a mistake.

You could make a *math* mistake, but don't worry, you won't get sent to Alcatraz. You'll just get a cute little form in the mail instructing you to correct the problem.

Give it a try. You might surprise yourself. Good luck!

The
Non-
Seminar

Odds and Ends

It took four hours for the dealer to realize that
Lisa Carr was her name, not her purpose.

If you've made it to this chapter, either you must be *really* smart by now, or you've skipped ahead. Either way, look at how many pages you've covered!

In the past five chapters, we've covered the subjects that we present in our seminars across the country, but in greater detail.

In addition to our seminar material, we've included a few extra "odds and ends" in this mini-chapter.

Don't treat these subjects like leftover potatoes. They're still interesting, but they just didn't fit into any of our seminar categories. We cover a bunch of different subjects:

- **moving**
- **auto insurance**
- **buying vs. leasing a car**
- **identity theft**
- **engagement rings**
- **buying paint**
- **alumni giving**
- **life insurance**
- **how to be happy**
- **disability etiquette**
- **voting**
- **Facebook**

Unless you plan on never getting married, always riding a bike to work, and living in your parent's basement, you should read on.

You're off to a new city, and you have to move. A stick in the eye might actually be more enjoyable than the moving process, but these few tips should make life a little easier for you.

Unless you've got a lot of money to throw around (or your company is picking up the tab), you should move yourself.

The national self-moving companies are:

Budget	800 462-8343
U-Haul	800 468-4285
Penske	800 222-0277

There are a few major rules to keep in mind when renting a moving truck.

Negotiate
Do not accept your first quote. Each rental company wants your business and will slash its prices to get it. Call everyone, get your best quote, and then try to get the other companies to improve. Use the line, "I'd really *prefer* to go with you, but ..."

Talk to the *local* office
You'll initially speak to the national office to get a quote. The national office can guarantee you a *rate,* but usually cannot guarantee you a *truck* (bizarre). *You need to call your local office to confirm that you have a truck.*

Reserve early
The days at the beginning and end of the month are usually busy times (as that's when leases end). If you reserve early, you'll have more options and better pricing.

A couple of other things that you should remember include:

Boxes are expensive (often $5 *per box*). If you buy them directly from the movers, they're even more expensive [insert evil laughter from moving company here]. Have a chat with your friendly grocery store owner to see if any boxes are being thrown away.

Also, if you've hired a moving company, the **boxes that *you* pack are *not* insured** in the move.

Everyone needs auto insurance. Here's the skinny.

Basic Types

Bodily injury liability: Pays for injuries you cause to someone else. This is required in most states.

Property damage liability: Pays for damages to someone else's car, mailbox, garage, or pool (another story for another day). This is required in most states.

Personal Injury Protection (PIP): Pays for injuries to the driver and passengers of your car. This is required in some states.

Collision: Pays for your car when you get in a wreck. If you own a clunker, don't waste your money with this coverage. You'll end up spending more money in coverage than the value of any damages.

Comprehensive: Pays for damage to your car due to theft, earthquake, raining frogs (name the movie), or other things not wreck-related.

Uninsured motorist: Pays for your injuries when you get into an accident with an uninsured motorist.

That "20/40/10" thing

Most insurance policies and state standards are written in a funny code with slash marks. This will help you translate.

First number (20): Up to $20,000 coverage for "bodily injury liability" (someone else's injury) per person injured in an accident.

Second number (40): Up to $40,000 coverage for "bodily injury liability" per accident.

Third number (10): Up to $10,000 coverage for all property damage per accident.

No-fault

Some states have something called **no-fault laws**. This means that your insurance carrier covers your bodily injury and property damage no matter who caused the accident.

Basically, the best choice between buying and leasing a car depends on the individual.

If you want a new car every three years, a lease might be best for you. A lease is simple, with minimal unknown costs. If you want to keep a car for a while, buying will save you money in the long run.

Before we start, you need to master the leasing jargon:

Residual value: Value of your car at the end of the lease.
Capitalized cost: Amount to be financed.
"Can't go lower": Lies. All lies.

Lease pros and cons

(+) Leases usually have lower monthly payments.

When you lease, you aren't paying for the whole car. Instead, you're paying for the difference in the car's value *now* versus its value at the *end* of the lease.

(+) Leases have no repair costs.

Since your car is new, it will be under warranty over the life of the lease. If you own a car, your warranty will eventually end.

(-) Leases have higher insurance premiums.

Since you don't own the car when you lease, the leasing company gets to call the shots when it comes to insurance. They usually require more than minimum state standards. Remember to factor in this cost when comparing choices.

(-) Leases have restrictions.

A lease charges you extra fees for driving too many miles. When you own, you can drive as much as you want.

(-) Lease payments never end.

If you lease a car and then lease again, your payments never end. When you buy a car, you'll eventually pay it off.

So, there are pros and cons for each. The choice is yours.

You can't actually steal someone's identity. Even John Travolta and Nicolas Cage couldn't pull off a stolen identity in that movie Face/Off, and they *literally switched faces*. A human with emotions cannot deny movie brilliance with lines like, "I don't know what I hate wearing worse: your face or your *body*."

Identity theft typically means using someone's personal information to steal money. Victims may not only lose money, but their credit history can be damaged.

College students and young graduates are highly vulnerable because of their high use of technology (file sharing, social networking sites, etc.), avalanche of credit card offers thrown into the trash, large use of social security numbers for identification, and low frequency of reviewing credit card and checking accounts. So what can you do?

Guard your information. Tear up all of your credit card statements and offers, ATM and gas receipts, and other personal documents. Keep your computer and wireless network password protected. Remember that others can hear you when you yell into your cellphone in a crowded place. And pay particular attention to protecting your **social security number** since this can open the door for bad guys to apply for credit on your good name.

Even if you're computer wise, you can get burned in low tech ways. "Dumpster diving" (going through the trash), "shoulder surfing" (criminals sneaking a peek at your credit card), and "skimming" (restaurant servers selling your credit card numbers) are common.

Monitor. The three credit bureaus are required by law to provide you a free credit report every year (see annualcreditreport.com). Also, review your credit card and check statements carefully each month.

Problems. If something goes wrong, request a "fraud alert" be placed on your file of the three major credit bureaus (Experian, Transunion, and Equifax). Tell them that you're an identity theft victim and be vigilant in clearing your name.

Before you start looking at engagement rings, we suggest you find that special someone. Here are the **four C's**:

Clarity: Clarity refers to the flaws, or **inclusions**, in the diamond. The naked eye cannot pick up any flaws until you drop to SI_2 on the scale.

Color: Color is labeled from D to Z (see the scale on the right). Diamonds appear more "yellow" as you move down the scale. At G-H-I, it is still difficult to notice any color when a diamond is mounted.

Cut: Cut refers to the angles and proportions of a diamond. Some popular shapes are **brilliant** (round), **emerald** (rectangular), **princess** (square), and **pear shape**.

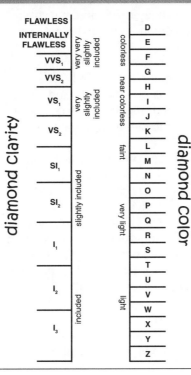

Carat: The weight of a diamond. For a brilliant cut, a .5 carat diamond is roughly 5.3mm across.

.5 carat   1 carat

If you're looking for good value, consider a diamond with SI_1 clarity and I color, since the flaws and color are not noticeable to the naked eye. If your girlfriend shops with a microscope, you might want to reconsider.

*Get a **certificate** when buying your diamond.* This prevents you from getting ripped off and provides you with all the vital data about your diamond. **GIA** is the leader in certifying diamonds.

It's time to paint your kitchen. You decide on the color blue and confidently head to your local paint store.

When you walk in, you say: "I'll take blue." And the clerk replies, "Would you like an interior oil-based semi-gloss?" And you say, "No, I'd like bluuuuuuee."

Well, a long time ago, someone decided to make paint complicated. We'll help you make sense of it all.

First, paints fall into two basic categories:

Latex (or water-based): Most of the liquid is water, so it dries quickly and is easy on clean-up. It's the most common type of paint.

Oil-based: As you might guess, most of the liquid is oil. It usually goes on smoother and covers more thoroughly in one coat, but it's harder to clean up and it stinks.

Then you have to pick your color. Unfortunately, "blue" comes in about 10 billion different shades. You'll be given some choices (displayed on a small card, or **swatch**) to help you decide. If the color "Dreaming of Clouds" speaks to your heart, then by all means, *follow your heart.* Your paint store won't have all ten billion choices on the shelf. Instead, your dream color will get mixed for you while you wait.

Your next step is to pick the right type of **finish.** Each color has five different degrees of shininess (see the arrow below). A gloss is easier to clean, so it may be good for a kitchen. A flat finish does not reflect too much light, so it may be a good choice for a ceiling.

Finally, if you're painting on drywall or making a big change in colors, you may need to apply a **primer** before you paint. Yes! More work!

Shiny				Dull
Gloss	**Semi-gloss**	**Satin**	**Eggshell**	**Flat**

If you're just coming out of school, giving money back to your alma mater, fraternity, or sorority is probably the last thing on your mind.

Actually, if you thought of the last thing on your mind, alumni giving might be just behind that.

Schools know that you're starting a new job or entering graduate school, buying a car, paying loans, or – put more succinctly – broke. Why, then, do they bother you, a new graduate, for a $10 or $25 donation?

They want your **participation,** even if it's small. Why?

Rankings. For better or for worse, many people judge the stature of a school based on the college rankings in *US News & World Report* magazine.

Five percent of a school's overall ranking in US News is based on "alumni satisfaction" which is based on only one factor: **percentage of alumni giving.** Since the giving rate is usually lowest in young alumni, increased participation can have a real impact on rankings.

Funding. Many colleges apply for grants from foundations that require a school to include its alumni giving participation in its application. More alumni giving participation can result in more grants for the school.

Participation not only helps the school, but it helps *you* as well. For the rest of your life, you're branded (on a place on your back that you can only see with two mirrors) as "a graduate of xyz school." Every time you apply for a job or your team wins a game, you're an xyz graduate to your friends and colleagues. A more "prestigious" school can increase the value of your degree.

Money adds up. Even if your giving is small, you'd be surprised at how quickly gifts in the $10 to $100 range add up. Giving helps bridge the gap between tuition received and the cost of running a school, which can be huge when you factor in financial aid, salaries, building maintenance, and so on.

"Life insurance? Yes, I love to talk about my death. Way to end the book on an **up** note, guys!"

Sorry. Let us state that none of our readers will *ever* die, but this will be helpful to tell your *friends* who don't have the book. Here are some things that *they* should know!

How does it work? Your **beneficiary** (the person you name in your policy) receives money (the **face amount**) if you die.

Who needs it? If you're a new graduate without a spouse or kids, it's really optional. But once you get married, then *game on*. You should make sure that your family is financially secure if you...r *friend* is no longer there with a paycheck.

There are two major types:

Term life. You're insured for a **term** (or length) of five years, ten years, or whatever. Term life is simple: if you die, it makes a payment. If you stop paying your monthly premiums or your term ends, you're no longer covered.

Whole life. You're insured for your *whole life* – it's "permanent" life insurance. This type of life insurance not only pays money when you die, but it includes something similar to a *savings account* in it. For this reason, whole life is usually more expensive than term life. As a new graduate, consider getting term life for its lower cost and simplicity.

Here are ways to get insurance:

Employer insurance. You may discover that you already have life insurance through your employer, but it's usually a fairly small policy (two to three times your salary).

Get your own policy. If you get your *own* policy, you'll probably be able to get a larger face amount than what you can get at your job.

Getting a policy *when you're healthy* usually protects your right to maintain life insurance, even when you're sick. If you wait and try to get a policy when you're on your deathbed, you'll probably be out of luck.

Look for life insurance through an agent or your alumni association.

How to be happy

Over the past few years, a bunch of smart people have spent increasing amounts of time studying the science of happiness. After reading a bunch of "happiness research" (start with an online search -- it's interesting), we're really happy (ha ha ha ha!) to share with you our findings.

To start, we all have a highly resiliant "baseline" happiness level. People who suffer great losses (blindness) or great gains (lottery) quickly return to their baseline level.

With that said, what makes people happy? Make your guesses before you read past the bold print.

Staying busy. Yep, staying busy helps. When you're engaged in an activity, rather than passively watching Grey's Anatomy (maybe a bad example for those rabid fans), you tend to be more happy.

Religion. No single religion claims the happiness trophy, but "religious" people tend to be happier.

Children. Nope. Surprisingly, there is little correlation of happiness to parenthood. Statistically speaking, kids might make you feel more comfortable about speaking of poop in public, but they won't make you more happy.

Money. Maybe. If you're so poor that you're worried about food and shelter, more money will make you happy. But, once your basic needs are met, more money will typically only make small, temporary increases in happiness.

Healthy relationships. Ding! Across almost every study, the best predictor of happiness is healthy relationships with family and friends, particularly satisfying marriages. On a similar note, sexual intimacy, more than just sex itself, has been shown as another strong predictor of happiness.

Comparisons. Finally, when we compare ourselves to others less fortunate, our happiness increases (and vice versa). So, appreciate what you have and tell all of your loser friends, "Thanks!"

At work and in your private life, you'll encounter people with disabilities (wheelchair user, blind, deaf, mental illness, etc.). Some simple rules of etiquette can help you from saying or doing something stupid that you might regret later (a good rule of life).

Don't lean on wheelchairs. Someone disabled in a wheelchair views it as an extension of his body. If you bump someone's chair (even if you don't bump the person), say "excuse me." If you lean on his chair, let him pull on your nose.

Speak normally. If someone is deaf, speak directly to him and not to his interpreter. And when you shout REALLY LOUD, you jump straight to the front of the idiot line.

Shake hands. If someone has an artificial limb or is missing a limb, offer to shake his hand. Using your left hand is ok.

Don't be overly helpful. The best way to find out if someone needs your help is to *ask*.

Be accomodating. If you're having a conversation with someone in a wheelchair, sit down to be at eye level (when possible).

Identify yourself. When speaking with someone with a visual disability, they may not recognize you with your fancy, new $2.99 cologne. Say, "Hey, Rico Suave here."

Be patient. When speaking to someone speech-impaired, listen attentively and be patient. Ask short questions that require short answers, and never pretend to understand if you don't.

Relax. If someone is disabled, it doesn't mean that he is easily offended. If you say, "See you later" to someone blind, let it go. If you ask someone in a wheelchair to go on a "walk to the park," correcting yourself with, "I mean, let's take a walk and a roll to the park" just makes things worse, and you jump to the front of the idiot line again.

Generally speaking, treat a disabled person as an independent adult like anyone else and you'll be good.

All around the world, voting is a pretty big whoop. Some people are pretty serious about voting. Other people are *really* serious.

In 1993, rebel guerrillas in Peru dynamited two buses on the day of elections to prevent people from voting. So people walked.

In 2004, Taliban insurgents distributed pamphlets threatening women with execution if they took part in Afghanistan's elections. And women still voted.

We could fill the rest of this book with examples like this, but if people risk their *lives* to vote and if women and African-Americans spent decades in this country for the right to vote, it's probably a whoop.

But it's not just an abstract whoop, your vote affects you on a very personal level. You elect people who affect your take-home pay, personal safety, streets, privacy, medical care, student loan rates, job prospects, and the air you breathe. Here's the scoop.

Register. To become an official voter, you need to register. It's usually as simple as filling out a one-page form, but the process varies a little from state by state (visit Vote411.org).

When you register, you're typically asked to join a **political party**.

You should think of each party as a "team" first and a set of beliefs second. Although parties have some basic ideologies, the tangled web of issues and policies can vary significantly with candidates and elections over time. Keep in mind that most people do not identify with *everything* in a specific party.

Republicans. These guys are often represented by their red color (on political maps), the term GOP (Grand Old Party), and their elephant logo.

Relative to Democrats, Republicans generally believe in lower taxes, less goverment (they want *citizens* to make more of their own decisions), and social conservative issues (stronger families).

Democrats. You'll often see these guys referred to by their blue color on political maps and their donkey logo.

Relative to Republicans, Democrats generally believe in progressive taxes (higher taxes for higher earners), *more* of a government role in citizens' lives (stricter gun control and more regulation on businesses), and liberal social issues (protecting the environment).

Outside of these two party gorillas (to stick with the zoo animal theme), there are a number of smaller parties. The **Libertarian Party** favors few restrictions on businesses and strong civil liberties (freedom of speech, religion, etc.) The **Green Party** advocates environmentalism and nonviolence.

Independents. If you choose not to pick a party, you may feel sad and alone during **primaries** (elections *within* a party) since you may not get to vote. For example, in many states, only registered Democrats were allowed to vote for Obama or Clinton in the primary for Democrats in 2008.

Voting place. Use Vote411.org to find your polling place (usually only minutes from your home and quick), but if you live in on-campus housing, you may need to send in an **absentee ballot** (also found on Vote411.org) to your *home state*.

Read. Many politicians court the stupid vote. Don't be part of this prized demographic. Newspapers and candidates' websites are a wealth of good voting information.

Vote. On election day, the "I Voted" sticker becomes the must-have fashion accessory. Everyone has one. The red and blue goes with almost any outfit and it gives the "I'm Responsible" vibe to friends. You'll not only get this sticker, but deep inside your heart, you'll know that *you're* a very big whoop.

facebook If you haven't heard of Facebook, ask your computer about the "information super highway." Some tips are below.

Privacy. There are about a billion privacy settings, but you need to learn how to use them. They'll help you (a) avoid weirdos and (b) get a job and keep it. Why?

Employers. Many employers review your Facebook profile prior to making a hiring decision. Really. They told us. So either clean up your page so that you feel comfortable for your mother to see it or get familiar with your privacy settings.

Employers also asked us to add something else to the book: **Don't use Facebook at work.** Does that imply that one should work at work? Sheesh.

Poking. Stop. If you poked someone in the real world, you'd get smacked. It's unnecessary.

Excess. Don't overload your profile page with unnessary applications. Who really needs to see a vibrating hampster? Actually, we love the vibrating hamster.

Real World. When "Facebook stalking," remember that the real world still exists. If you meet this person, pretend not to know everything about him/her. "Creepy" is never a good first impression.

When meeting someone new in "real life," do not run back to your computer to *friend* them. You must wait at least a day.

Friending. Facebook is not a game to see who has the most friends. This is not MySpace. *Do not friend random people.* Instead of just hitting the "add friend" button, reply with a friendly note. "Hi! Tell me again how I know you?"

Photos. Do not put up a picture of yourself drinking and everyone should keep their shirts on. If you don't have a picture loaded (the infamous question mark), you will be considered ugly by default.

And once you use LinkedIn instead of Facebook, you'll know that you're officially an adult.

If any particular page in this book bores you, please refer to one of the following jokes to lift your spirits:

Two guys walk into a bar. You would think that the second one would have ducked.

or

A ham sandwich walks into a bar. The bartender says, "Sorry, we don't serve food here."

or

A priest, a rabbi, and a monk walk into a bar. The bartender says, "What is this? A joke?"

401k A company-sponsored plan that allows you to save your money (just like you normally would) with a bunch of added perks.

alcove Partly enclosed area connected to a room.

APR Annual percentage rate. An interest rate that factors in to all loan fees.

ARM Adjustable-rate mortgage. The interest rate will change over time.

back-end load Mutual fund fee charged when you withdraw money from a fund.

balanced fund A fund with a mix of stocks and bonds.

beneficiary The recipient of funds from your life insurance policy if you die.

blue-chip stock Stock from a large company that has "rewarded" shareholders well in the past.

bodily injury liability Car insurance that pays for injuries you cause to someone else.

bond An IOU issued by a company or government.

brilliant cut Round diamond.

Bringing it in The money you earn (interest) when someone else uses your money.

carat (engagement rings) Weight of a diamond.

CD Certificate of deposit. Pays better than savings, but money is in prison.

checking account Secured account where you can keep money and write checks. You have easy access to it, but you rarely earn interest.

clarity (engagement rings) Flaws in a diamond. SI_2 is still unnoticeable to the naked eye.

closing costs The fees that you'll have to pay when you sign the papers to buy your house.

collar stay The little things that go in a shirt collar to keep it from turning up.

collision Insurance that pays for damages to your car caused by a wreck.

color (engagement rings) Clear is more expensive. Yellow is less expensive. "I" is still unnoticeable to the naked eye.

comprehensive Insurance that pays for damage to your car (not wreck-related).

co-payment A small fee you pay every time you visit a doctor.

debit card A payment card where money is withdrawn from your account (like a check).

deductible The dollar amount you need to pay before the insurance kicks in.

deduction Any tax break besides a mouth to feed.

dependent A certain dollar amount used in your tax return (a mouth to feed).

DIA Stock that tracks the Dow Jones Industrial Average.

dividend Periodic payments made by some companies to stockholders.

down payment Money that comes out of your pocket up front to buy a house.

emerald cut Rectanglar diamond.

equity The value in your home that's yours.

ETF Exchange traded fund (e.g., DIA, QQQQ, or SPY).

exemption The term used when you claim yourself as a dependent.

expense ratio A pay-as-you-go mutual fund fee (applies to most funds).

FHA loan A government-backed mortgage that allows for smaller down payments.

FICA tax Medicare plus social security tax (7.45%).

filet mignon Usually the most tender and expensive (per ounce) cut of steak.

flex account Short for flexible spending account. Helps reduce your medical payments through non-taxed dollars.

four o'clock position Position of silverware on your plate to signify that you are finished with your meal.

front-end load Mutual fund fee charged when you put money into the fund.

GOP Short for "Grand Old Party," or Republican political party.

grace period, student loan Amount of time after you graduate before you have to start repaying your loan.

gross income The "Money You Make" pile.

growth fund A fund composed of growing companies (usually more high-risk).

hanger rule For women dressing business professional, both the top and bottom of an outfit must come from the same hanger.

health savings account (HSA) Health insurance plan with a special checking acct.

HMO Health maintenance organization.

host The person who initiates a meal. Follow his or her lead during a business dinner.

income fund Fund with established companies that make periodic payments to shareholders (dividends).

index A group of stocks used to track the market (Dow Jones, Nasdaq, and S&P 500).

index mutual fund A fund that tracks an index.

IRA Individual retirement account. A way to save for retirement with tax benefits.

itemizing Listing your "tough times" and "good deeds." If greater than your standard deduction, you should itemize.

large-cap stock Stock that represents a large company.

liability insurance Insurance for when someone sues you for an accident (plus that person's bills).

liqueur Sweetened alcoholic drink.

load Fee for owning a mutual fund.

load fund A fund with a front- or back-end load.

Maitre D' Your welcoming presence at a restaurant.

maki (rolls) Raw fish (or something edible) wrapped in rice and seaweed.

matched 401k A 401k for which an employer will match employee contributions.

Medicare 1.45% tax. Largely used to pay the sick bills for your grandma.

money market fund Safe investment with many perks (higher rates, check writing).

mortgage A loan to buy a house.

mortgage insurance A fee to protect your lender from your running off to Ecuador.

mutual fund An investment that is composed of various stocks, bonds, etc., bundled into some kind of group or category.

mutual fund manager Person who makes investment decisions for a particular fund.

no-fault laws Your insurance carrier must pay no matter who caused the accident.

no-load fund A fund with no front- or back-end loads (will still have an expense ratio).

nonvintage wines Wines with no vintage (year) on the label. Grapes are from a few different years.

on-line broker Company that executes on-line buy and sell orders for stocks, funds, etc.

out-of-pocket maximum The most you'll have to pay for a medical bill. Insurance picks up the rest.

part-year method A way to keep your money and earn interest if you work only part of a year.

PCP Primary care physician. The family doctor that you have to visit before you can see a specialist (in most HMOs and POSs).

pear shape cut Teardrop-shaped diamond.

P/E ratio Price of a stock divided by its earnings, or the company's profit. (The higher the P/E, the more "expensive" the stock.)

personal injury protection (PIP) Insurance that pays for injuries to the driver and passengers of your car.

porterhouse steak Filet plus NY strip.

POS Point of service insurance plan.

PPO Preferred provider organization.

pre-existing condition A medical condition you have prior to signing up for insurance.

premium The monthly payment you make to carry any type of insurance.

primary care physician See PCP.

prime rib Same cut of meat as the ribeye, but prepared differently (slow-cooked).

princess cut Square diamond.

Glossary

principal The amount you owe on a loan.

residual value Value of your car at the end of a lease.

retirement accounts Ways to save for retirement with tax benefits (e.g., 401k, IRA, and 403b).

ribeye steak Same cut of meat as the prime rib, but prepared differently (grilled).

rolls (maki) Raw fish (or something edible) wrapped in rice and seaweed.

sashimi Raw fish without the rice.

savings account Low-interest investment.

sector A group or industry. (Many funds are divided up by sector.)

short loin Where most good cuts of meat are found in a cow.

small-cap stock Stock that represents a small company.

Social Security 6.2% tax. Largely used to pay the bills for your grandma.

sommelier See wine steward.

spread-style shirt A shirt with no buttons on the collar.

SPY Stock that tracks the S&P 500.

stock Part ownership of a company.

studio A one-room apartment or one room connected to a kitchen.

subsidized student loan The government pays the interest on the loan while you're in school. Celebrate good times.

sushi Raw fish over rice.

taxable income The "Money They Tax" pile.

term life Life insurance for a set period of time.

T-bone steak Filet plus NY strip.

Uncle Sam A cartoon representing the US government.

uninsured motorist Insurance that pays for your injuries when you're in an accident with an uninsured motorist.

W-2 form Your financial report card sent by your employer at the end of the year.

W-4 form That stupid tax form that you get on your first day at work.

walk-up An apartment with no elevator.

wasabi Green, spicy horseradish.

whole life Combination of life insurance and an investment.

Index

Index

Index

Feedback from our readers

We thrive off your feedback. The content in our seminars, book, and starter kits is a collection of feedback from students, recent graduates, professionals, and everyone in between.

If during your read of this book, you feel inspired to share a story, suggestion, or comment, please send it our way at:

Feedback@CapandCompass. com

No comment is too random. To underline this point, read two of the submissions that we received recently.

– The team at Cap & Compass

Cap & Compass,

Let me first say what an excellent book you have put together. It is truly a fun read with wit and sarcasm dripping from every page.

However, nobody is perfect. I am willing to make a suggestion with no expectation of compensation.

Page 22: "Oh Sherry" is not a Journey song, but a Steve Perry song from his self-titled solo album – SHAME on you.

Sincerely,
Roy
St. Thomas, USVI

Hello,

I picked up a copy of the book *life after school. explained.* from the office of my boss. I think you have done a great job with the book.

However, I do have one nitpicking point: Chuck the cow on page 34 should probably be Chuck the bull, or Chuck the steer.

Cows are female.

It's a little thing but, coming from Texas, knowing the difference in livestock is an essential trait.

Cheers,
Russell
San Antonio, TX

Want to buy one of our books?

Shipping Address:

Name_____

Address_____

City_____ **State**_____ **Zip Code**_____

Phone number (if there is a problem)_____

E-mail (for confirmation)_____

Billing Information (if paying by credit card) [Visa, MC, Disc, or Amex]

Name on card (exactly) _____

Credit Card Number_____

Expiration Date _____

Billing Zip Code_____

You can buy this book:

ONLINE
www.CapandCompass.com

BY PHONE
1-866-LIFE-EXPLAINED
(1-866-543-3397)

BY MAIL
Just fill out the form on the left.
See back for instructions.

LARGE QUANTITIES
Go online for bulk discounts
of five or more copies.
Choose to customize the book
and give it as a thoughtful gift
from your institution.
See our site (or call)
for more information.

Great for high school grads:

the college years   _____ x $12.95   = _____

Graduating with God:
for high school graduates   _____ x $12.95   = _____

Great for college grads:

life after school. explained.   _____ x $12.95   = _____

Graduating with God:
for college graduates   _____ x $12.95   = _____

Shipping ($3.00 + $.50 for each additional book)   = _____

Sales tax 6% (only for FL)   = _____

Total   = _____

Please send a check,
money order, or
credit card information
(please do not send cash) to:

Cap & Compass
1005 Pine Lake Cir
Palm Beach Gardens, FL
33418

Please allow two weeks for delivery.